FROM COVER TO COVER

BRIAN L. HARBOUR

BROADMAN PRESS
Nashville, Tennessee

4222-41
ISBN: 0-8054-2241-2

Dewey Decimal Classification: 252
Subject heading: SERMONS—COLLECTIONS
Library of Congress Catalog Card Number: 81-7197
Printed in the United States of America

Dedicated to
Daniel Vestal,
George Gaston,
and
Ken Smith—
Brothers in the Ministry

ACKNOWLEDGEMENTS

All Scripture passages marked NASB are from the *New American Standard Bible.* Copyright © The Lockman Foundation, 1960, 1962, 1963, 1971, 1972, 1973, 1975. Used by permission.

All marked NIV are from *The New International Version New Testament.* Copyright © 1973 by the New York Bible Society International. Used by permission of Zondervan Publishing House.

All marked RSV are from the Revised Standard Version of the Bible, copyrighted 1946, 1952, © 1971, 1973.

All quotations marked AMP are from *The Amplified Bible,* New Testament. Copyright © 1954, 1958 by The Lockman Foundation. Used by permission.

All Scripture verses marked KJV are from the King James Version.

All quotations marked TEV are from the *Good News Bible,* the Bible in Today's English Version. New Testament: Copyright © American Bible Society, 1966, 1971, 1976. Used by permission.

Verses marked TLB are taken from *The Living Bible.* Copyright © Tyndale House Publishers, Wheaton, Illinois, 1971. Used by permission.

Preface

Evangelicals have long been known for believing the Bible "from cover to cover." Oddly enough, few of us preach the Bible from cover to cover. When was your last series of sermons on Leviticus? Or the Song of Solomon? How much preaching have you done from Jude? Or Lamentations?

Most preachers are probably like me. I spend considerable time in the Gospels and in the Epistles of Paul. That's where most of my pulpit performance is focused. Once in a while I will take a hike through Hebrews or jump into James or plunge into the Psalms or interpret Isaiah. Most of the time, though, I stay on familiar ground.

If, however, we believe in the Bible *from cover to cover* we ought to preach the Bible *from cover to cover*. If we believe *all* of Scripture is *the* Word of God, then we should seek to communicate all of its truth.

In our day there is a deep hunger in all denominations and Christian groups for the Word of God. "Is there any word from the Lord?" is a question frequently asked. We do have a Word from the Lord in the Bible, in *all* the Bible.

In this book I have presented a sermon idea from each book of the Bible. Each is chocked full of illustrations and quotable quotes. This is not an attempt to solve our neglect of the whole Bible but to "prime the pump" for you as you seek to broaden the biblical base of your pulpit ministry. Let's not merely believe the Bible from cover to cover. Let's preach it!

A special word of appreciation goes to Mrs. Nelma Camp, my outstanding secretary, for her tireless work on the manuscript. And my deep gratitude to my wife, Jan, who provided the inspiration to see this project through.

BRIAN L. HARBOUR
Pensacola, Florida

CONTENTS

Old Testament

New Testament

OLD TESTAMENT

GENESIS

1. A Portrait of God

Genesis 1

In all of literature there is no passage in any book which compares with the sublimity, simplicity, and splendor of this first chapter of Genesis. One scholar has called this chapter "the most amazing composition in all the world's literature," for here, using only seventy-six different word forms, the author arranged in a precise poetic pattern this portrait of the beginning of our world.

This chapter describes the creation and introduces the creature. The focus, however, is on the creator. If you would circle with a pencil the word *God* each time it is used in the first two chapters of Genesis, you would discover its presence forty-six times. In both chapters, God is the primary subject.

According to G. A. Studdert-Kennedy, an English chaplain in World War I, life's basic question is, "What is God like?" He visited a wounded soldier in a hospital. "What I want to know," said the officer, "is what is God like? I never thought about it much before the war. I took it for granted. But now it is different. When I'm transferred into a new battalion, I want to know what the Colonel is like. He bosses the show, and it makes a lot of difference to me what sort of chap he is. Now I'm in the battalion of humanity. I want to know what the Colonel of this world is like."[1]

What is the Colonel of this world like?

Many answers to that question are given today. From the child who said, "God is greater than Superman, Batman, and Spiderman put together" to Paul Tillich, who spoke of God as the "ground of all being," many pictures of God are presented.

Notice what we learn about God in this beautiful portrait in Genesis 1.

1. *The Existence of God*

"In the beginning God . . ." Those are the first four words of the Bible. No attempt is made to explain God. There is no effort to prove His existence. When the biblical writer pulled apart the curtains of past history and peered as far as he could see into the sacred antiquity of the dawn of our universe, there God was.

2. *The Oneness of God*

What a contrast to the pantheistic consciousness of the other cultures of that day. Many gods adorned the pantheon of Babylonian, Egyptian, and Assyrian believers. By contrast, in the Book of Genesis we see a picture of one God who stands entirely alone. There is no pantheon of lesser deities. No female principle stands as his counterpart. He is alone God.

3. *The Creativity of God*

Some scientists and computer experts were determined to discover the mystery of creation by the aid of a complex computer. Research was done. Information was fed into the computer. The magic moment arrived. As the computer readout emerged, on it was written one simple sentence: "See Genesis 1." That's good advice, for it is here that we must turn for information about the creation. What does the Bible affirm? That God created the world. However it came about and whenever it happened, God did it.

4. *The Sovereignty of God*

The word of God was all that was necessary to bring everything else into existence. God is not a part of nature; he created it. He is not a part of history; he started it. Everything is pictured as being under God's divine control.

A legend about Abraham's childhood tells how Nimrod sought to kill him because a vivid star appeared in the sky when Abraham was born. Abraham was concealed in a cave, and his life spared. It was there in the cave that Abraham first encountered God. He peered from the cave, across the face of the desert, and saw the sun rising in all its glory. "Surely the sun is God!" Abraham exclaimed, and he worshipped the sun. At evening, when the sun sank into the west, Abraham said, "This must not be God, for the Author of creation cannot set." At night he saw the moon and stars. Abraham exclaimed, "The moon must be God, and the stars are his host!" He worshipped the moon. Daybreak came, however, and the light of the moon was gone. Abraham concluded, "These heavenly bodies must not be gods, for they obey the law. I will worship Him who imposed the laws upon them."[2]

God the Creator, the one who imposed the laws upon all of creation, is sovereign over all.

5. *The Involvement of God*

The word *brood* is the word of *motherhood*, of a mother lovingly watching over her children. It pictures a hen with outspread wings under whose protective care she will gather her chicks.

A piece of graffiti declared, "God isn't dead. He just doesn't want to get involved!" Nothing could be further from the truth. God, sovereign and omnipotent over all, chose to become involved in the affairs of this world. He is not only a God of power but also of passion, a God whose infinity did not prevent his involvement.

6. *The Greatness of God*

The overriding impression of the creation account is that the Creator is a great God. He is a God in the light of whose greatness all other light seems to be darkness by comparison.

At the funeral of King Louis XIV of France, the great cathedral in Paris was packed with mourners paying final tribute to the king whom they considered to be the greatest king who ever lived. The cathedral was dark except for one lone candle which illuminated the golden casket that held the mortal remains of the monarch. At the appointed time, Massillon, court preacher, stood to address the assembled clergy of France. He arose, walked over to the pulpit, reached down, and snuffed out the one candle which had been put there to symbolize the greatness of the king. Then in the darkness he spoke just four words: "God only is great!"

EXODUS

2. A Church That Gives

Exodus 36:1-7

After he called a special meeting to discuss the rundown condition of the church, the pastor asked for pledges from the leadership of the church. The chairman of deacons declared, "I'll give five dollars." At that moment a piece of plaster fell from the ceiling and hit the deacon on the head. "Make that fifty dollars," he quickly replied. Lifting his eyes toward heaven, the preacher prayed, "Lord, hit him again!"

What a different picture in our text. God had a task for the Hebrews to do. They were to build a tabernacle in which they could worship him. It would take so much, and they seemingly had so little. But look what happened. When the people took seriously their responsibility to give, the resources were so abundant that Moses finally had to tell them to quit giving. Can you imagine that! Have you ever been on a finance committee that had to send out a notice to the people to quit giving? Have you ever pastored such a church?

How did it happen?

1. *Everyone Gave*

When Moses presented God's instructions for the people to give, the Bible says, "All the people went to their tents to prepare their gifts" (Ex. 35:20, TLB). The reason for their success was that everyone gave. That was the first key. The problem in our churches today is that we have too many of our members who never give anything.

Adlai Stevenson told of a pastor who so moved one of his congregation that the man jumped to his feet and cried, "Oh Lord, use me—in an advisory capacity." That typifies the reaction of too many of our members today. They want to be a part of what is happening, but they do not want it to cost them anything. They want it to be in an advisory capacity.

Why do Christians not give? The problem is our attitude. We have been influenced by the selfishness of the world. We have allowed the clanging symbols of secularism to drown out the voice of our Master who said, "It is more blessed to give than to receive" (Acts 20:35, TLB).

At the heart of the Christian faith is the spirit of giving. A pastor wrote to one of his laymen with an appeal to participate in a financial campaign. The man responded negatively with the comment, "It seems to me that you preachers have come to interpret Christianity as give, give, give." The pastor responded to the man's letter, "I thank you for the finest interpretation of Christianity I've ever heard. It is give, give, give. It seems to have begun at Calvary when God gave his Son for us."[3]

A church that has an overabundance of resources is one that catches the true spirit of Christianity. It is a church in which everyone gives.

2. *Everyone Gave What He Had*

The second key was everyone gave as he was able. There was no matching of gifts, no mold into which everyone had to fit, no mumbling because some gifts were more valuable than others. Some gave jewelry (35:22), some fine clothes (35:23), others silver and bronze (35:24), others fine-twined linen (35:25). Everyone simply gave what he had.

Everyone's part is important. Whether you are a child with a small allowance, a young person with a part-time salary, a young couple struggling to get started, a single adult living on a single salary, a senior citizen living on a pension, or an executive pulling in lots of skins—your part is important, and your part is missed if you do not give.

A thirteen-year-old boy named Robert Hill lived in Italy where his dad was stationed in the army. When he read about Albert Schweitzer's work in Africa, he wanted to help. He had enough money to buy one bottle of aspirin. Then he wrote the Air Force and asked them if they were passing over Africa, he wanted them to drop the bottle of aspirin down to Dr.

Schweitzer. A radio station learned of his story and publicized it. Before long, the spirit of his attitude spread. Eventually, he was flown by the government to Schweitzer's hospital along with four and one-half tons of medical supplies worth $400,000 freely given by thousands of good-hearted people. When Dr. Schweitzer heard the story, he said, "I never thought one child could do so much."[4]

The key to overabundance in the resources of the church is for each to say to God what Peter said to the blind beggar, "Such as I have I give" (Acts 3:6).

3. *Everyone Gave God Top Priority*

These believers also put priority on their giving. God did not get the leftovers. He did not get second best. They gave God their best (Ex. 12:5). They gave God his first (34:19).

Many do not give to God's work because of confused priorities. They simply do not have anything left after they have taken care of the expenses of the affluent life-style which they have chosen to live. They surround their lives with luxuries and give God the leftovers.

Our attempt to emulate the life-style of the world has added such pressure on our personal expenses that, when it comes time to give a little money to God's work, we ask, "How little can I give?"

When God is given top priority in our finances, overabundant resources for the church will result.

4. *Everyone Gave in Response to God's Grace*

Why did the Hebrews do all of this? They gave because their hearts had been stirred by the spirit of God (35:21). They gave in response to what God had given them. When they realized again what God had done for them, they gave freely (35:22), regularly (36:3), and generously (36:5).

When I look again at this amazing incident, when I see a people so caught up with what God was doing in their midst that they gave an overabundance of resources to carry it out, my deepest prayer is, "Oh, Lord, do it again in us."

LEVITICUS

3. What Does a Preacher Do?

Leviticus 9

A friend used to tease me with this comment: "I thought about being a preacher when I was young, but I decided not to because I don't believe in working on Sunday. But," he would add with a twinkle in his eye, "it sure must be nice to work just one day a week!"

A speech teacher was asked by a young man what it would take to become a good preacher. She said, "Fill your mouth with marbles and practice speaking. Take the marbles out of your mouth one by one; when you lose all your marbles, then you'll be a preacher."

What is a preacher? Someone who works only one day a week? Someone who has lost all his marbles? No. A preacher is a man God has called and set aside for the work of the ministry. Paul told Timothy, "If any man aspires to the office of overseer, it is a fine work that he desires to do" (1 Tim. 3:1, NASB).

But what does a preacher do? One of the clearest New Testament answers to that question is found in 1 Timothy 4:6-16. An Old Testament parallel is Leviticus 9. In the description of the consecration of the priest we see clearly outlined the demands and duties of the man of God.

1. *The Demand*

No other calling is as demanding as is the role of pastor. The role of the minister in today's world is multifaceted in its character. Administrative ability, eloquence in the pulpit, availability to the congregation, counseling skills, adaptability to all age groups, evangelistic fervor—all must be in the repertoire of those preachers who keep pace with the expectation of their parishioners. And sometimes, there are simply not enough hours in the day.

What essential ingredients will enable the pastor to meet the demands placed upon him? Two are apparent in our text.

The first demand is a *consecration of will*. This is the decision stage. Moses outlined what God demanded of Aaron in order for him to be anointed as priest. Aaron had to accept the stipulations. He had to come to the point where he could say, "I hereby choose to do what God is asking of me." He had to consecrate his will.

Before he was nineteen years of age, Jonathan Edwards had listed some seventy resolutions in his diary which he kept religiously. At the heart of these resolutions was the following: "Resolved: that every man should live to the glory of God. Resolved second; that whether others do this or not, I will." Some such consecration of our will to the will of God is essential for the preacher of the gospel.

I remember when I came to that point of commitment in my personal pilgramage toward the pastorate. As a high school senior, God began dealing with me. My plans were to enter the field of medicine. When I began to sense God leading me toward the pastorate, I had to do some serious reevaluation. My pastor, Clyde Lee Herring, spent many hours with me helping me to clarify what was happening in my life. A youth-led service provided the opportunity for us to test the waters. My first sermon which I preached in that youth service was preceded by days of prayer to God that he would give some indication of his will. The movement of God in the service was obvious. His purpose for my life was clear. The following week I shared with the congregation, "God wants me to be a preacher." To God I said, "I'll do what you want me to do." That consecration of our will to the will of God is the initial demand on a preacher.

Holiness of life was also demanded of the man of God. The overriding spirit of our text is that of cleansing and purification. The purpose of the sacrifices which were so meticulously carried out was to wash away any iniquity which would prevent the priest from being acceptable in the sight of God.

God does not require a beautiful vessel nor a large vessel. He does, however, demand a clean vessel. There must be nothing in our lives to detract from the good news which we are to proclaim to the world.

To be a preacher of the gospel, our will must be consecrated and our life must be clean.

2. *The Duty*

What does a preacher do? What are his duties? Notice the clear answer given in our text.

The duty of the man of God was *intercession*. He was to take the petitions and needs of the people into the presence of Yahweh. This was symbolized by the priest's breastplate on which the names of the tribes of Israel were engraved. As the priest went into the presence of God, he literally carried the names of his people on his heart (Ex. 28:21,29).

Prayer must be at the heart of a pastor's ministry. Said one man in the past: "The conclusion of the whole matter is, that while study makes an instructive preacher, and eloquence makes an attractive preacher, it is much secret prayer which makes an effective preacher."[5]

W. E. Sangster tells of a black preacher who gave this explanation of his approach to preaching. He said that he "read himself full" and "thought himself clean" and then "prayed himself hot."[6]

The product of preaching without prayer is powerless patter from the pulpit. A praying preacher will be a powerful pulpiteer and pastor.

The duty of the man of God was also *interpretation*. Not only was he to take the needs of the people to God but he was also to communicate the truth of God to man. This was symbolized by the Urim and the Thummin (Lev. 8:8) by which the priest discerned the will of God.

Nothing a pastor does is any more important than his charge to communicate to the world the unsearchable riches of Christ. The man of God must first discover what God's Word says. Then he must communicate this message in such a clear way that it feeds the hearer. Sangster's description of the preacher as a "spiritual chef" is altogether appropriate.[7] To break the Bread of Life to a hungry world, that is the duty of a man of God.

Because communication is the primary purpose of the preacher, clarity is a top priority item. After a seminary student had preached his carefully prepared and eloquently delivered sermon in preaching class, he anxiously awaited his professor's response. The professor said, "You can't convince your congregation that God is great and that you are great in the same sermon."

To clearly communicate the Word of God—that is the duty of the preacher.

A third duty is implied but not stated. The duty of the man of God was *inspiration*. The priest was to be an encourager who repeatedly recalled the people to their faith in God. His job was to take the hands of his people and put them in the hand of God, so they could walk in his power.

Someone has suggested that a preacher is a doctor of divinity who gives "faith-lifts." May it ever be so.

NUMBERS

4. Reminders

Numbers 15:37-41

Have you ever forgotten something? Traditionally, we attribute forgetfulness to the absentminded professors. The truth of the matter is that forgetfulness is an experience with which we are all familiar. Even preachers forget.

One young pastor was talking with an older minister about the challenges he would face in the ministry. One challenge that especially fascinated the young pastor was the wedding ceremony. He listened carefully as the older minister outlined each step he should take. In conclusion, the wise advisor suggested, "If you ever forget what to say, just quote Scripture. It is always appropriate at a wedding."

Shortly thereafter the young pastor had the opportunity to test his newly gained knowledge when a young couple requested that he perform their ceremony. Everything went according to plan until the point in the service where the young pastor pronounced them husband and wife. At that point, his mind went blank. He could not remember what to say next. Suddenly, the advice of the old pastor came to him: *Quote Scripture*. Unfortunately, the only Scripture that came to his mind which he dutifully quoted was, "Father, forgive them; for they do not know what they are doing" (Luke 23:34).

We often complain about our bad memories. However, we could not exist for a single day without this God-given ability to forget. To have to experience the accumulated pain of all our previous days would be overwhelming. To have to experience the intensity of all our past failures and trials would be more than any of us could bear. Our ability to forget, therefore, is one of the blessings of life.

Like most blessings it is a mixed one, for the ability to forget also creates some problems. There are some things we need to forget. Other ideas, lessons, and teachings need to be remembered. This is where our forgetfulness creates problems for us.

It is this negative side of forgetfulness that God addressed in our text. God had richly blessed the Hebrew people and had invited them into a special covenant relationship with him. He would be their God, and they would be his people. On his side, he promised continued protection. On their side, he demanded obedience to the stipulations which he had carefully outlined for them in the Ten Commandments. God knew, however, that they would easily forget these laws. So he ordered Moses to put tassels on their robes and a blue cord around the tassels, "So you shall remember and do all my commandments" (v. 40, RSV). The tassels were to be reminders of the love of God for them and the demands of God upon them.

When Jesus left his disciples, he knew that they, too, would soon forget his offer of grace and his call to discipleship. Therefore, he too gave them reminders. These reminders are before us as we come to the Lord's table to share in his special meal. The bread and the wine, like the tassels on the robes of the Hebrews, are to remind us of our Savior. Jesus told the disciples that as often as they partook of the Lord's Supper, they did this "in remembrance of me" (1 Cor. 11:24, RSV).

What do the elements of the Lord's Supper remind us of?

1. *The Life of Jesus*

The bread and wine, representing the body and blood of Jesus, remind us first of all of his life.

A little boy came to the dinner table only to be told by his dad, "Go wash your hands. There might be some germs on them." As he headed for the bathroom the boy mumbled, "Germs and Jesus. Germs and Jesus. That's all we hear about around here. And you can't see either one of them!" Because we do not see Jesus in the flesh, it is easy to forget his claim on our lives. These elements of the Lord's Supper serve as reminders that he was a real person who lived a real life in a real place at a real time in history. They remind us of his life.

The symbolism goes even deeper. As we partake of the wine and bread, we are symbolizing the fact that this Jesus who once lived on the earth now lives within us. This truth was expressed by Jesus in the closing hours of his physical life. "If anyone loves Me," Jesus said, "he will keep My word; and My Father will love him, and We will come to him, and make Our abode with him" (John 14:23, NASB). This truth was explained by Paul in his letter to the Galatian churches. "I have been crucified with Christ," Paul said, "and it is no longer I who live, but Christ lives in me" (Gal. 2:20, NASB). And it is experienced by every believer of every age. "Christ in you, the hope of glory" (Col. 1:27, NASB). That is the eventual outcome of the life of Christ which these communion elements symbolize.

2. *The Love of Jesus*

The bread and wine also remind us of his love. Jesus did not just live on the earth. He also died, and the Bible proclaims that he died for us. We can all understand the statement in John's Gospel: "Greater love has no one than this, that one lay down his life for his friends" (John 15:13). Jesus' love went even deeper than that. It caused him to lay down his life for his enemies. In a day of casual Christianity, we need to be constantly reminded of the costliness of Jesus' love.

A request was made of Dwight L. Moody while he was in England preaching a crusade. The request was to visit a man who had been an invalid for years. As he entered the man's house, he expected to find a depressed man who lived under the gloom of his handicap. Instead, he found the man to be vibrant and full of life. After a long visit, Moody asked the man, "Don't you ever get discouraged, having to lie here like this all day long, week after week?" "Yes," the man replied, "I do get discouraged. Whenever discouragement descends upon me, the devil comes in, walks over to my bed, and whispers in my ear, *Does God really love you, letting you suffer like this*? Whenever that happens," the man continued, "I just grab old Satan by the neck and drag him over to the foot of the cross. I make him look at Jesus dying for my sins. And I ask him, *Doesn't he love me*?"

Here before us are symbols of the body and blood of Christ, a body which was broken and blood which was shed for us. They are reminders of his love.

DEUTERONOMY

5. Choose Life

Deuteronomy 30:19-20

The Easter service at a church in Mississippi was interrupted a few years ago by an unexpected guest. In the middle of the service a man entered the church with a gun in one hand and the leash attached to a German shepherd dog in the other hand. He ran to the front of the auditorium, shot his dog, and then took his own life, all in full view of the astonished worshipers and the television audience.

What a pity for life to be so empty, so void of meaning, that a man would choose death over life! As I heard about this tragic experience the question came to me: What is it that gives life its meaning?

Is it pleasure? Some think so. One modern man has suggested that the principle aim in life after age sixteen should be comfort. That is the *Playboy* philosophy, and it permeates society today.

This is no new idea, however. Jesus' story about the rich farmer revolves around this idea (Luke 12:16-21). The farmer majored in pleasure. He thought he had it made. But God called him a fool.

Is education what gives life its meaning? Some think so. One successful businessman was asked, "Did you graduate from Harvard?" "No," he replied, "but five hundred of my two thousand employees did!" Education is important, but it is not what gives life its meaning.

Is physical beauty what gives life its meaning? Many think so today. Plastic surgery, silicone injections, and Grecian formula are all a part of our drive to look young. Jesus clearly declared that it is what's inside that counts (Matt. 12:35).

What then does give meaning to life? What must a person do to follow the admonition of our text to choose life rather than death?

1. *A Purpose to Live For*

The first key is a purpose to live for. This is the only antidote for an empty life. Such a purpose is probably man's primary need in our day.

Listen to well-known psychiatrists who speak to this matter. Carl Jung claims that "the central neurosis of our times is emptiness." Rollo May, New York psychologist, says, "On the basis of my clinical practice, as well as that of my psychological and psychiatric colleagues . . . the chief problem of people in the middle . . . of the twentieth century is emptiness." Victor Frankl echoes their claims: "The state of inner emptiness is at present one of the major challenges to psychiatry."[8]

How do we counter this blight of emptiness that is upon us? The key is to determine a purpose for your life. A successful person in any field is a goal-oriented person. We may not make our goals, but as is commonly stated, our goals will make us.

2. *A Positive Attitude to Live By*

When the goal is set, we must then pursue that goal (or goals) with a positive spirit. The power of positive thinking is more than a theme made famous by Dr. Norman Vincent Peale. It is a secret to a full and abundant life.

The greatest accomplishments in life have been the things that people claimed could not be done. In the fifteenth century, people believed that a person could not sail west from Europe and reach the Far East. While people were busy declaring it could not be done, Columbus did it. Later it was said that human beings could not fly, that if God wanted humans to fly, he would have given them wings. While people were touting the impossibility of it, the Wright brothers did it.

A positive attitude of expectancy grounded in a God "who is able to do exceeding abundantly beyond all that we ask or think" (Eph. 3:20, NASB) is what enabled Paul to declare, "I can do all things through Him who strengthens me" (Phil. 4:13, NASB). That same power source is available to each of us.

3. *A Persistence to Live With*

The third ingredient in a successful life is the persistence to remain at the task. Paul Harvey once said that if anyone asks him the secret of his life he would respond: "I get up when I fall down."

The reason many miss out on what life has to offer is that they turn and leave the dock before their ship comes in.

4. *A Person to Live For*

In addition, a full life comes when we have a person to live for. The Old Testament expression of this truth is in our text: "loving the Lord your God, obeying his voice, and cleaving to him" (v. 20, RSV). The New Testament equivalent is found in the words of Jesus: "And as Moses lifted up the serpent in the wilderness, even so must the Son of Man be lifted up; that whoever believes may in Him have eternal life" (John 3: 14-15, NASB). Life is found in Christ. You choose life, therefore, when you choose to follow him.

5. *Conclusion*

An eccentric millionaire was looking for a new executive assistant. He gathered all his junior executives to his mansion where he showed them a shark in his swimming pool. "The first man to jump in and swim across the pool will become my executive assistant," he said, "plus, I will give him a bonus." After a few seconds the millionaire's butler hit the water, swam across, and barely made it out the other side. In amazement the millionaire said, "I'll go inside and write out your bonus check." The butler responded, "If it's all the same to you, sir, first of all I'd like to get the guy who pushed me in."

Nobody is going to push us in life. We have to make the choice ourselves. If we will get a purpose to live for, a positive attitude to live with, a persistence to live by, and a person to live for, then we will experience the life for which God created us.

JOSHUA

6. Claiming God's Future

Joshua 1:1-11

In a *Peanuts* cartoon strip, Linus shared with Charlie Brown his dreams for the future. "When I get big," Linus says, "I'm going to be a real fanatic." Charlie responded, "What are you going to be fanatical about?" With an uncertain look on his face, Linus replied, "Oh, I don't know . . . it doesn't really matter . . . I'll be sort of a wishy-washy fanatic!"[9]

With the Promised Land out before them, it was no time for the Hebrew people to be wishy-washy fanatics! The demand was for single-minded devotion to the plan of God.

The poignancy of the scene in the first chapter of Joshua cannot be fully understood unless you remember a scene recorded earlier in Numbers 13, for this was not the first time the Chosen People stood at the threshhold of their Promised Land. Forty years earlier they had been in the same place with the same opportunity before them. However, fear, pessimism, and negativity prevented them from taking possession of the land at that point.

Now the opportunity was once more before them. The faltering and fearful leaders of the past were buried beneath the rocky soil of the wilderness. A new generation had come to maturity. A new leader was raised up before the people. The land was before them, and the challenge was given, "Arise, go over the Jordan, and take possession of the land."

How like the challenge confronting us today. The church stands on the threshold of the promised land. Never before has there been a greater openness to the gospel. Never before have we had available the tools to proclaim the whole message to the whole world as we have them today. The time is ripe for a bold mission thrust!

In the story of how these early people of God claimed their Promised Land, we can learn some lessons on how to face the challenge before us today.

1. *Proper Preparation*

Notice in the first three chapters the elaborate plans Joshua made before the people took their first step. He ordered the people to prepare sufficient food (1:11). He sent spies to analyze the challenge presented by Jericho (2:1). Instructions were given to the priests (3:6). A challenge was issued to the people (3:9). Every step was carefully planned. Joshua knew that enthusiasm had to be channeled through proper preparation.

What must we do to prepare for God's future?

We must analyze the need. Ralph Neighbour uses the term "target groups." A careful study of the neighborhood in which we live will reveal these target groups which need the touch of Christ.

We must assess our resources. Every church has a reservoir of spiritual gifts bestowed by the Holy Spirit. Every congregation has people with special skills. A careful study of our membership will reveal the resources available to meet the needs around us.

Then, we must activate our people to use those resources and dedicate those gifts to minister to those needs. Moving our people out of the passive voice into the active voice is the greatest challenge of our day.

A paraphrase of an oft quoted statement would suggest that we pray as if everything depended on God; then, plan as if everything depended on us.

2. *Complete Commitment*

Notice also that claiming God's Promised Land was contingent upon the complete commitment of the people. An important principle weaves its way through each episode in the Book of Joshua. The principle can be simply stated: Obedience brought victory, but disobedience brought defeat.

This principle is most clearly illustrated in the contrast between chapter 7 and chapter 8. Deliberate disobedience led to defeat (chap. 7). Complete commitment led to victory (chap. 8).

The presence of sin in the lives of Christians will deprive us of the power of God just as it did for the Hebrews. Complete commitment is the channel through which God's dynamic power is released in our lives.

I was recently greeted at home with the announcement that the vacuum cleaner did not work. That was a trauma of magnificent proportions. Why? Because on a scale of one to ten, my mechanical abilities rate a minus two. I checked the belts. I investigated all the parts. Then an inspiration hit me. I removed the hose and looked through it. No light came through from the other end. With a broomstick I pushed the guilty culprit out, a clump of dust and debris which prevented the vacuum cleaner from working properly.

That is a parable of life. God's power is often thwarted in our lives because of clumps of dirt that we allow to remain. The kind of commitment that causes us to come clean with God releases the flow of God's power in our lives.

3. *Total Togetherness*

Success also demanded a unity of purpose among the Hebrew people. Before crossing the Jordan, the tribes of Reuben and Gad, and the half-tribe of Manasseh requested permission to settle on the east side of the Jordan. Joshua agreed, on one condition. These tribes must first cross the Jordan with the others and participate in the capture of the land (1:12-17). Joshua realized that the task before them demanded the total efforts of all the people blended together in a unity of purpose.

Two ministers in a small town were openly critical of each other's efforts and constantly opposed one another. After a joint meeting in which they planned a community-wide effort, one took this parting shot at the other, "We'll just go out from here and continue to do the Lord's work, you in your way and I in his."

With the task before us we must be willing to rise above "my way" and "your way" and combine our resources in moving forward "his way." "United we stand, divided we fall" is more than just a timeworn phrase. It is the key to our future success in the work of the Lord.

Our future is as bright as the promises of God. With preparation, commitment, and togetherness, we can claim God's future!

JUDGES

7. He's Got Charisma!

Judges 6:1 - 7:25

What is a leader? Much debate has recently centered around this question. Many definitions have been offered, but all seem to fall into two basic categories.

Some describe a leader in terms of what he is. This is the trait approach to leadership. In this understanding a leader is a person who has certain qualities such as empathy, persuasiveness, insight, and courage which establish his leadership.

Others describe a leader in terms of what he does. This is the functional approach to leadership. In this understanding, a man is a leader who can produce results for the group better than anyone else.

The Book of Judges focuses on several individuals who emerged as leaders of Israel between the time of Joshua's death and the selection of Saul as king of Israel. The title "judge" is rather misleading, for the primary role of these leaders was not judicial but military. These leaders were not elected by the people but were chosen by God. They had charisma!

Gideon was one of the greatest of these leaders of Israel, and in our text we see the ingredients of his leadership.

1. *His Compulsion*

Verse 11 pictures Gideon at work, beating out wheat in the winepress in order to save it from the Midianites. This task might not seem significant. The important point is that Gideon was doing something. He did not have to receive a letter from the pastor to encourage him. He did not have to have a special Sunday set aside to get excited. He did not have to see the crowd going with him. He took the initiative himself. Gideon was compelled, not from outward circumstances, but from inner character to do what he could for God and his people.

Several years ago Coach Bud Wilkinson delivered a series of lectures on physical fitness in support of the president's physical fitness program. In Dallas, a reporter asked him, "Coach, what would you say is the contribution of modern football to physical fitness?" Expecting some elaborate answer, he was unprepared for Wilkinson's response. The coach answered, "Absolutely nothing." The reporter stared, squirmed, and finally stuttered, "Would you care to elaborate on that?" "Certainly," Coach Wilkinson replied, "I define football as twenty-two men on the field who desperately need rest and fifty thousand people in the grandstands who desperately need exercise."

That is also a picture of the church, a few compulsively active people running around the field while the mass of people rest in the pews. A leader is one who has the compulsion to get out of the grandstands into the game.

2. *His Commitment*

While Gideon was busy at work, God called him for a special task. Like all of us, Gideon initially felt inadequate to the task. Notice his outline of inadequacies in verse 15. He said that he was of the tribe of Manasseh, which was the lowest and weakest tribe in all Israel. Then, he said that his family was the lowest and weakest family in the tribe of Manasseh. Further, he was the lowest and weakest member of his family. Thus, he was the lowest and weakest member of the lowest and weakest family of the lowest and weakest tribe of all Israel! You cannot get much lower than that. To this exposition of excuses, God gave a single reply, "I will be with you."

What is most apparent in verses 12-24, however, is not Gideon's caution but his commitment. The preparation of a sacrifice to offer to God was a symbol of the commitment of his life. Gideon was saying to God what Bobby Richardson said in a prayer, "Dear God, Thy Will. Nothing less, nothing more, nothing else. Amen." Gideon had been busy; now he was busy for God. He was compelled to do something; now that compulsion was channeled into commitment to God.

Someone has suggested that the most important fact about a person is not how busy they are, but how they are busy. A person with unchanneled compulsion is like the man who "mounted his horse and rode off in all directions." A leader is one who, like Gideon, is committed.

3. *His Courage*

Having committed his life to God, God now revealed to Gideon what he wanted him to do. He wanted him to tear down the altars to Baal and Asherah and reestablish an altar to Yahweh. Verse 27 (NASB) says, "Then Gideon took ten men of his servants and did as the Lord had spoken to him."

Was Gideon afraid? Yes, the Bible clearly says so. Verse 27 tells us that because Gideon was afraid, he carried out God's command at night rather than in the day. Gideon was afraid, but he was not controlled by his fear. He overcame it in commitment to God. Courage, says one definition, is being the only one who knows you are afraid! Courage means acting not in the absence of fear but in the midst of fear.

What was the source of his courage? According to tradition, the Goths always went over their battle plans twice: once when they were sober so they would not lack skill and thoroughness, and once while drunk so they would not lack courage and daring. Gideon's courage did not come from spirits but from the Spirit of God. Verse 34 says, "So the Spirit of the Lord came upon Gideon." His commitment to the Lord was the source of his courage.

4. *His Conquest*

Chapter 7 tells the exciting story of the conquest of Midian by Gideon and his army. Surrender to God's will and God's way led to success. Valor led to victory. Commitment led to conquest. Gideon won the victory for the Lord.

In a day when we so often encourage each other in mediocrity, we need to remember that "in all these things we overwhelmingly conquer through Him who loved us" (Rom. 8:37, NASB). In a time when most Christians limp feebly from one defeat to another, we need to remind ourselves that God "gives us the victory through our Lord Jesus Christ" (1 Cor. 15:57, NASB).

Many descriptions are used of Christians in the New Testament. At first they were called "followers of the way." Then, at Antioch they were called "Christians." The commonest word for those committed to Jesus is "disciple." In his epistles, Paul addressed the Christians as "saints." John, in his epistle, suggested another name for Christians: "overcomers." He wrote, "For whatever is born of God overcomes the world; and this is the victory that overcomes the world, our faith" (1 John 5:4, RSV).

When you move out in faith for God, when you commit yourself to him, when you courageously take your stand for him, you can win the victory. You do not have to be defeated by Satan. You do not have to be disgraced by sin. You do not have to be destroyed by suffering. You do not have to be distracted by sensuality. You can win the victory. You can overcome.

A key point in the narrative of the conquest is made in verse 2. God said to Gideon, "The people who are with you are too many for Me to give Midian into their hands, lest Israel become boastful, saying, 'My own power has delivered me.' " The victory is not in the performance of man; it is in the power of God. As Paul put it in his epistle to the Philippians: "I can do all things through Him who strengthens me" (Phil. 4:13, NASB).

A famous entertainer once said, "I'd rather be a failure in a business I love than a success in something I didn't love." The good news of God's Word is that you can be a success at something you love, when you've got charisma!

RUTH

8. The Searching Single

Ruth 3—4

Singleness as a life-style is becoming increasingly popular in our day. About one-third of the adults in contemporary America are single. Some are single by choice, like the man who described a bachelor as someone who never made the same mistake once! Others are single by circumstances, having been initiated into the ranks of the formerly married through divorce or the death of a mate.

Are all singles looking for a mate? No. Some are single and liking it. They opt for singleness for personal, economic, or professional reasons. Many, however, are marking time in their single state. Singleness is a temporary resting place from which they hope to launch into marriage. These are the searching singles.

At a Sunday night song service, the minister of music told the congregation to pick a hymn. One single lady began pointing to men in the congregation saying, "I'll take him and him and him." Another single shared her favorite verse in a testimony service: "If any man would come after me, let him!" (I missed the Scripture reference on that verse.) These are examples of searching singles.

Ruth fits into the category of searching singles. She had married a young Jew whose family had moved to Moab to escape the difficult economic situation in Israel. Her husband's name was Mahlon. After only a short time, Mahlon died. When Ruth's mother-in-law, Naomi, decided to return to her home, Ruth chose to go with her.

Back home in Israel, Naomi filled the role of cupid in the

attempt to find another husband for Ruth. Boaz was the selected target. Chapters three and four in the Book of Ruth show how she chased Boaz until he caught her.

In her search she provided some insight for searching singles today. When you are single, and looking, what should you do?

1. *Avoided Self-Pity*

Naomi was burdened by self-pity. She complained that the hand of the Lord had gone against her (v. 20). She even wanted to change her name to Mara (bitterness) to publicly and permanently express her grief. Naomi bathed in self-pity, but there was no hint of it in Ruth.

Ruth, of course, had every reason to feel sorry for herself. Life had not been easy for her. She chose instead to face her problems with energetic hope and optimistic expectation. Ruth captured the spirit expressed by some unknown writer of our day:

"Today upon a bus, I saw a lovely maid with golden hair. I envied her—she seemed so gay—and wished I were so fair. When suddenly she arose to leave. I saw the cruel braces as she hobbled down the aisle: a victim of polio was she. But as she passed—a smile she gave to me. Oh, God, forgive me when I whine. I have two straight feet. The world is mine!

"And then I stopped to buy some sweets. The lad who sold them had such charm. I talked with him. He said to me: 'It's nice to talk with folks like you. You see,' he said, 'I'm blind!' Oh, God, forgive me when I whine. I have two eyes. The world is mine!

"Then walking down the street, I saw a child with eyes of blue. We stood and watched the others play. It seemed he knew not what to do. I stopped a moment, then said: 'Why don't you join the others, dear?' He looked ahead without a word, and then I knew he could not hear. Oh, God, forgive me when I whine. I have two ears. The world is mine!

"With feet to take me where I'd go, with eyes to see the sunset's glow, with ears to hear what I would know—Oh, God, forgive me when I whine. I'm blessed indeed. The world is mine!"[10]

Everybody has problems in life, married people as well as singles. You cannot determine what will happen to you in life, only how you respond to what happens to you. You will determine the quality of your singleness by whether or not you are able to avoid self-pity.

2. *Took Care of Herself*

A second key in Ruth is that she was careful to keep herself as appealing as she could be. When Boaz came to the field, he noticed Ruth. A loose translation of his response is: "Wow! Who is that girl?" (2:5). There was something about Ruth that caught the eye of Boaz. Was it her physical beauty? Perhaps. More likely, it was a beauty of character that caused her to outshine the other workers.

The word Ruth is a contraction of the Hebrew word *reuth*. This Hebrew word might come from the root that means "something worth seeing." In this case, Ruth's name could be a reference to her beauty. There is another root from which the Hebrew word might come. This root means friendship. In this case, Ruth's name could refer to her amiable and affectionate disposition. In either case, the point is the same. There was something about Ruth that made her attractive to Boaz. She took care of herself.[11]

If you are single, and looking, ask yourself a question. Is there anything about you that would make someone want to marry you? Physically, emotionally, spiritually, socially, and vocationally—are you developing yourself into the person that you ought to be?

3. *Stayed Involved in Life*

There is a third key to Ruth's successful search. She stayed involved in life. She avoided the tendency to withdraw. Notice in chapter 1 that Ruth refused to leave Naomi. Whether it was the spirit of adventure or her allegiance to Naomi's God which prompted the moving response in verses 16 and 17, we cannot tell. In either case, what is clear is that Ruth refused to drop out of life. She was ready to move into the future.

Then notice what Ruth did in chapter 2. Because she and Naomi had no food, she immediately pursued the only course available. She went out to glean in the fields. A time-honored tradition in Israel was to leave some of the crops unharvested for the poor and the widows. Ruth took advantage of this tradition. In the daily duties of carrying out her work, she met the man who was to be her future husband.

Many singles ask me, "Where can I meet an eligible man or woman?" That's not an easy question to answer. But I am sure of this much. You will never meet a person who might possibly be a remarriage partner for you if you check out of life. Go to work. Get involved in a church with a single's group. Take advantage of the legitimate services for the formerly married in your city. Play tennis. Get on a ball team. Join a ceramics class. Become a part of a bowling league. Go back to school. Get involved in life. Quite often you will discover, as Ruth did, that in the daily activities of living, your path will cross with the man or woman who is right for you to join in a new venture in the world of the married.

4. *Conclusion*

A preacher said to one of the older single adults in his church, "I heard you are getting married." "It's not true," responded the lady, "but thanks for the rumor."

Some singles are not thankful for the rumor, for they are happily single. But for those who are searching, here are some principles that will help you to be prepared: avoid self-pity, take care of yourself, and stay involved in life.

1 SAMUEL

9. Facing Today's Giants

1 Samuel 17:1-52

The Bible is full of exciting stories about young people. There was Moses' sister whose faithful watching helped preserve Moses' life and made possible the fulfillment of God's plan (Ex. 2). There was young Joseph, showing the strength of his inner convictions in the midst of unpleasant outer circumstances (Gen. 37). There was John, designated by the title "the disciple Jesus loved," who was probably still a teenager when Jesus called him to be his disciple. There was young Timothy to whom Paul wrote, "Let no one look down on your youthfulness, but rather in speech, conduct, love, faith, and purity, show yourself an example of those who believe" (1 Tim. 4:12, NASB).

Perhaps the most famous youth of all was young David. His most significant accomplishment as a young person was when he faced, fought, frustrated, and finished off the giant Goliath. The story is told in 1 Samuel 17. David was still a very young man, a teenager, for Goliath was insulted that this kid with a ruddy complexion would come out to fight him (v. 42). I'm not sure what "ruddy" means in this context. It could be a reference to complexion problems! So here was this little kid with pimples, facing a giant who was over nine feet tall. What a ludicrous situation that was!

I believe this is a perfect picture of the situation facing young people today. The problems which young people face loom large before them like the giant did before the young David. What are these giants?

Drugs is certainly one of them. We are living in the chemical age. Of course, we did not invent drugs. Neither did Timothy Leary or the Rolling Stones. Marijuana dates back five thousand years to the early Hindu shrines in India. Heroin was mentioned on cuneiform tablets of ancient Mesopotamia. Speed can be traced to the Ma Huang plant from ancient China. In the eleventh century a Persian radical named Sheik Hasan ibn-al-Sabbah used a concentrated form of marijuana to induce his followers to carry out assassinations and terrorist activities.

We did not invent drugs. They have been around a long time. But in our day the chemical bomb has exploded. They are avilable to everyone at almost any time. The universal availability of drugs is what makes them one of the giants looming before youth today.

Another giant is *alcohol*. Teenagers are constantly challenged to grab for all the gusto they can get. Again, this is no new problem. Egyptian carvings over six thousand years old show men being carried home drunk by their servants. This was Noah's problem, as well. As far back as Plato, the subject of alcohol and youth was a matter of public concern.

And it still is. Ninety percent of high school youth admit to having had a drink. Sixty percent have been drunk. There are one hundred thousand preteen alcoholics in our country. The adverse effects of alcohol are hidden behind the scintilating scenes of suaveness which urges us to do what the cool people do. Alcohol is the number one drug problem facing youth today.

Sex is another giant that young people face. Although "everybody is not doing it," the fact is that teenage sex is on the increase. Recent statistics indicated that 40 percent of the girls in the United States between fifteen and nineteen years of age are sexually active.

One father told his daughter to follow the directions on the mayonnaise jar: "Keep cool, but don't freeze." Unfortunately, the pressures are so great that this advice is hard for a teenager to follow. Sex is one of the giants that loom before young people today.

Like the giant Goliath who towered above David, so these giants tower above young people today. Is the situation hopeless? No! For David followed a pattern that enabled him to win the victory over the giant.

1. *He Dared to Be Different*

Not only did David have to overcome the threat of the giant. He also had to overcome the pressure of his peers. The Bible says that all of Israel was afraid of the giant (v. 11). When the men of Israel heard the challenge of Goliath, they fled (v. 24). But notice the response of David. "For who is this uncircumcised Philistine, that he should taunt the armies of the living God?" (v. 26*b*). David was not swayed by the feelings of the group or by the pressures of the crowd. He thought for himself. He dared to be different.

The peer pressure to conform to the crowd and to give in to these giants complicates the problems for youth today. There is a tremendous pressure on young people to be like everyone else. Sometimes the pressure is subtle.

Several years ago when I lived in Atlanta, I drove down Peachtree Street where a group of hippies were demonstrating. They were carrying around signs which said, "Down with Conformity." Everyone of the signs were identical. All the hippies wore their hair the same way. They were all dressed the same way. They all talked the same way. They all thought the same. They all smelled the same. They were conforming in their nonconformity.

Satan is proclaiming with more success today than ever before one of his best lines, that conformity will insure acceptability. If you are like everyone else, he proclaims, if you do what everyone else does, you will be accepted. That is a lie. Respect comes not when you are like everyone else but when you consistently stand up for what you believe.

God is looking for individuals who will dare to be different, who will dare to do his will instead of the world's, who instead of being conformed to the world will be transformed from within by the Spirit of God.

2. *He Prepared Himself*

David did not go into the challenge empty-handed. He was prepared. He discarded the armor of the soldiers for it was too heavy. Instead, he picked up five smooth stones from the brook and put them in his pocket as ammunition to feed into his trusty slingshot. He was ready.

One of the greatest needs for Christian young people is to prepare to meet the temptations of the world. How can you prepare? By a decision and by discipline.

Proper preparation for the giants facing us today is the prior *decision* that we are going to opt for the right, whatever happens. The reason so many youth are defeated by the giants facing them is that they wait until they get into a situation to decide whether or not they want to do God's will. It is too late then. The commitment to God's way needs to be settled before the temptation comes.

The other key ingredient in our preparation is *discipline*. What we do in an emergency is merely the result of what we have been doing in the uneventful days which preceded the challenge. Therefore, a daily discipline to prayer, Bible study, service, and sharing is the best preparation for facing today's giants.

3. *He Kept His Eyes on God*

David knew he was no match for the giant in his own strength. But he did not face the giant in his own strength. He had the power of God in his arsenal. "You come to me with a sword, a spear, and a javelin," David said, "but I come to you in the name of the Lord of hosts, the God of the armies of Israel, whom you have taunted" (v. 45, NASB).

The Israelites looked at Goliath and said, "Look how much bigger he is than us." David looked at him and said, "Look how much smaller he is than God." They said, "He is too big to hit." David responded, "He is too big to miss."

Tom Dooley, one of God's greatest missionaries, faced unbelievable obstacles and opposition as he shared his faith. When asked how he kept going, he responded, "I remind myself of who is really keeping score."

When we realize that we never face any battle alone but that we have available to us the very power of God, when we understand that "greater is He who is in you than he who is in the world" (1 John 4:4, NASB), when we grasp the truth that God is keeping the score, then we can say to the giants of our day what David said to his, "Come on, you big ugly Philistine. God and I are going to get you!"

2 SAMUEL

10. Why Is the Son of the King Haggard?

2 Samuel 13:4

Amnon, the son of David, had a lot going for him. At his disposal were all the riches of the kingdom. His father was the most famous and powerful man in the land. In addition, the possibility existed that Amnon would someday succeed his father. What a happy young man this should have been. The biblical portrait depicts him, however, not as a man of joy but in the depth of despair, overshadowed by sadness.

A question was asked him by a friend, "Why is a son of the king haggard?" The question carries with it the implication that Amnon certainly should have been happy. He had every reason to be. He had been exposed to all the privileges, prestige, and power that went along with his position as the king's son. He was a son of the king. He should have been happy.

As Christians we, too, are sons of the King; not just any king, but God, the maker and sustainer of the cosmos. The testimony of Romans 8:16 (NASB) is, "The Spirit Himself bears witness with our spirit that we are the children of God." As Christians, we are part of a Kingdom that can never be shaken. Through faith we are making investments that will pay their dividends through all eternity. We have been established in a new relationship with God. If anyone ought to be happy, we should be, for we are sons of the King. Like Francis of Assisi, known as the apostle of joy, we should experience real joy in Jesus.

1. *The Interference*

With all that was at his disposal, with every reason to be happy, Amnon was nevertheless in despair. To discover what interfered with the joy he should have experienced will help us understand why joy so often alludes us today.

Sinfulness interfered with Amnon's happiness. Amnon raped his sister, defying the laws of God and man. This incident in Amnon's life is probably indicative of his general life-style. If so, we can conclude that his life was characterized by an indifference toward God that led at many points to specific acts of sin. The weight of that sin squeezed the happiness out of his life.

The most unhappy person in the world is not a person outside the family of God. The saddest person is one who is in God's family but who is carrying in his life the burden of guilt over sins he knows he should not have committed.

Another interference was *selfishness*. Amnon put self at the center of his life. Amnon's one concern was to fulfill his own selfish desires. He did not care what Tamar wanted. He gave no thought to David's feelings or Absalom's reaction. He did not care what tradition dictated. He wanted something for himself, and he took it.

God is a self-giving God, and the character of God is reflected in the universe. When we act otherwise, when we approach life in selfishness, we are at cross purposes with God and his universe. The result is unhappiness.

Amnon looked haggard because he centered his world in himself, and that's a mighty small package.

2. *The Implementation*

What then can be done? How can we overcome the haggardness which selfishness and sin cause and discover once more the joy of our salvation?

The first step is to *surrender to God*. God has a plan for every life. His plan is best. You will never find a real, enduring happiness until you have committed yourself to doing God's will for you.

Remove sin from the center of your life and put God there. Replace the declaration "I want" with the question, "What does God want?"

A second step that leads to joy is *service to mankind*. Albert

Schweitzer once said, "I don't know what your destiny will be, but one thing I know: The only ones among you who will be really happy are those who will have sought and found how to serve."

Remove self from the center of your attention and put others there. Replace the declaration "I need" with the question, "What do others need?"

Two roommates in medical school finished their course of study and went in opposite directions. One young man settled into a lucrative practice in a large city in the midwest. He enjoyed all the benefits of affluence. The other doctor, drawn by a great need about which he had learned, went to Africa and established a practice in a densely populated area. Years passed. One day the doctor practicing in America took a tour of Africa and included on his itinerary a visit with his former colleague. The American doctor was appalled at the conditions under which his friend worked. After the missionary doctor completed a surgery, his visitor asked, "How much would you have received for performing that surgery in America?" "Oh, I don't know. Maybe $2,000, maybe more." "And what did you get here?" The missionary doctor replied, "A few pennies and the smile of God!"

When the smile of God is on our lives, then we will experience the true joy of our salvation.

3. *Conclusion*

A lady was miserable as she shivered in the stands at the football game. The man behind her had spilled his beer on her favorite blouse. She was nauseated by the popcorn from the concession stand. The man in front of her kept getting in her way. She was freezing to death. And her team was forty points behind. Turning to her husband she said, "Honey, tell me again how much fun we're having."

When your life is characterized by surrender to God and service to others, you'll not have to ask that question, because Jesus' joy will be in you, and your joy will be full (John 15:11).

1 KINGS

11. Real Wisdom

1 Kings 3:5-14

Albert Einstein's genius was so unique that his name has become synonymous with intelligence par excellence. On one occasion he was on a lecture tour from university to university where he discussed his theory of relativity. Einstein did not drive, so he had a chauffeur who drove him from place to place. As they were driving along one day the chauffeur said to the brilliant scientist, "You know, I've heard this lecture so many times now that I could give it myself." Einstein accepted the challenge. "The people at the next university have never seen me," said Einstein, "so they won't know who I am. You put on my clothes and I'll wear your uniform and cap. You introduce me as your chauffeur and I will introduce you as Dr. Einstein."

Everything went according to plan. The chauffeur delivered the speech on relativity flawlessly. Einstein, sitting at the back of the lecture hall, enjoyed it immensely. Then, something happened that the two had not planned on. The moderator said, "We have fifteen more minutes, just enough time for some of you to ask Dr. Einstein a question." A mathematics professor asked a complicated, technical question involving mathematical formulas and language the chauffeur did not understand. Lacking the intellectual knowledge, he nevertheless had the practical wisdom to get out of the jam, for he responded to the question like this: "Sir, the solution to that problem is so simple that I am really surprised you would even ask me to answer it. Anybody can answer that simple question. To prove it, I am going to have my chauffeur come up and answer it!"

Never has there been such a need for wisdom, both intellectual and practical, as in our day. As much new knowledge has been developed in the last year as had been discovered in all of civilization before that time. In addition, we are faced with daily decisions that we must make which will greatly affect our lives.

A little boy at church misunderstood the words of a familiar hymn. He sang, "Wise Up, O Men of God." He was confused about the song, but clear about the need for mankind in our day. The need for wisdom has never been more urgent than it is today. From another man whose name is synonymous with wisdom, Solomon, we can gain some insight into what real wisdom is.

1. *The Supremacy of Wisdom*

Can you imagine the situation in which Solomon found himself? The God who owned the cattle on a thousand hills, the God who held the whole world in his hands, said to Solomon, "Ask what you wish me to give you." This was another way of saying, "What is the most important possession in life that I could put in your hands?"

How would you answer that question? If God told you that He would give you whatever you desired, what would it be? God suggested some standard answers to that request in verse 11.

Some would ask for long life. One Jewish man at age 105 quit going to church. He said that he figured God had forgotten about him, and he didn't want to remind God! Perpetuity is nice, but it is not the ultimate goal of living. Putting years to our life is not nearly as important as putting life to our years.

Some would ask for riches. A little boy was praying one night. He said, "Lord, please give me enough money to buy an elephant." His father overheard and asked, "Son, what would you do with an elephant if you had one?" The boy replied, "Who wants an elephant? I only want the money." Possessions are necessary ingredients in our day, but they are not the ultimate goal of living. Having the things money can buy is not nearly as important as having the things that money cannot buy.

Some would ask for power, for this is what God meant in the phrase, "nor have you asked for the life of your enemies." To have your enemies defeated is to have your own position and power exalted. Position in life is important, but it is not the ultimate goal for living. Knowing the adulation of our peers is not nearly as important as experiencing the affirmation of God.

Solomon had the opportunity to ask of God whatever he wanted. Solomon did not ask for perpetuity, possessions, or position. He asked for wisdom. Supreme among the values of life is real wisdom.

2. *The Source of Wisdom*

Where can this wisdom be found? The experience of Solomon reveals the answer to this question. Real wisdom comes from God. This was the promise made by James in his epistle: "But if any of you lacks wisdom, let him ask of God who gives to all men generously and without reproach, and it will be given to him" (Jas. 1:5, NASB).

Many other avenues for wisdom are being given priority today. Often we listen to the voices of men rather than to the voice of God, only to discover what one young man discovered. He had a sick mule and didn't know what to do. So he called his uncle Joe who once had a mule. "Uncle Joe," asked the young man, "didn't your mule get sick one time?" "Yep," replied Uncle Joe. "What did you do?" "I fed him turpentine," Uncle Joe responded. The young man took some turpentine and gave it to his mule. And the mule died! He immediately picked up the phone and called Uncle Joe. "I thought you told me that you fed your sick mule turpentine," he thundered over the phone. "Yep," Uncle Joe responded, "I did." "I took your advice, and it killed my mule." "Yep," said Uncle Joe, "killed mine too!"

You cannot believe everything you hear, for the wisdom

that comes from men is unreliable. True wisdom comes from God.

3. *The Scope of Wisdom*

Solomon ranked wisdom as life's greatest value. Real wisdom, he understood, could only be given by God. But what was the scope of this wisdom? What would this wisdom enable Solomon to do? The answer is announced in verse 9. Solomon wanted wisdom so that he could "discern between good and evil."

In his description of true wisdom, the first characteristic James pronounced in his epistle was purity (Jas. 3:17). "Real wisdom," James said, "is pure." The Greek word James used is a word which means "pure enough to approach deity." Real wisdom results in holiness of living. It enables a person to "discern between good and evil."

The ultimate result of wisdom is described in the Proverbs:

> Wise men store up knowledge,
> But with the mouth of the foolish, ruin is at hand.
> The rich man's wealth is his fortress,
> The ruin of the poor is their poverty.
> The wages of the righteous is life,
> The income of the wicked, punishment (Prov. 10:14-16, NIV).

2 KINGS

12. The Dynamic Discovery

2 Kings 22:3-11

King Josiah came to the throne of Judah in extremely perilous times. For fifty-five years, King Manasseh had led Judah down the road of carnality and wickedness. Designated by historians as the worst of Judah's kings, Manasseh had opened the floodgates of Judah to all manners of evil. It was a day of corruption in the land of Judah.

Amon became king after Manasseh's death. His brief reign, however, brought no respite from the wickedness of the day. It was only when young Josiah was brought to the throne that better days began to dawn. Spiritual renewal was already under way early in Josiah's reign, but it was the dynamic discovery of a book in the Temple one day which caused the kindling embers of renewal to blaze into the flame of revival.

What was this book? Scholars suggest it was a major part of the book of Deuteronomy which had been hidden in the Temple. We don't know for certain. What we do know is that the book discovered was some portion of Scripture which represented the written Word of God to man. This rediscovery of God's written Word brought the king to his knees in worship and evoked a breath of righteousness in the land.

Like Judah, America has been led down the road of carnality and wickedness. Elton Trueblood has said that the tragedy of our day is not that Americans are living by the wrong moral standards but that many no longer believe there are moral standards. The only hope for our nation, as it was for Judah, is to rediscover the Bible as God's written Word to man.

1. *Loved*

We need to rediscover the Bible as a book to be loved. God's people have always loved his Word. The Jewish scribes loved the Scriptures so much that whenever they made a new copy of it, they destroyed their old copies to protect them from base uses or neglect.

The early church loved the Word of God so much that they chose at times to go to death rather than to deny or destroy it.

Preachers of the gospel through the centuries have loved this Book. One of W. A. Criswell's childhood friends made fun of him by calling him a "little ole Bible reader." W. A. punched him in the nose! But he didn't stop loving this Book.

It is in the Word of God that philosophy has found its most profound inspiration, history its most thrilling chapters, and the human spirit its greatest encouragement. It is no wonder the psalmist declared, "How sweet are Thy words to my taste! Yes, sweeter than honey to my mouth" (Ps. 119:103, NASB). The Bible is not just another book. It is the Word of God.

2. *Liberated*

We also need to rediscover the Bible as a Book to be liberated. How often do we misunderstand the power of the Word of God and treat it as a fragile piece of china that needs to be protected. How often do we underestimate the inherent strength in Scripture.

That is what happened to God's Word in Judah. Scholars suggest that some well-meaning priest hid the book of covenant in the Temple lest it should be destroyed. What was the result? For sixty years Judah went from bad to worse. But notice what happened when God's people quit hiding the Word of God and set it loose to do its work (chap. 23). The king was convicted, the nation revived, and immorality defeated.

Someone has suggested that the Bible must be the Word of God to have endured such bad preaching over the centuries! It has endured bad preaching and more. As the hammer blows of criticism, scholasticism, and skepticism have been directed toward the Bible, the Word of God has proven to be an anvil which has worn out many a hammer.

The Bible does not need to be coddled nor protected. It needs to be set free. When we dare to liberate the Word of God in the world, then it will move with the power of a two-edged sword to convict, convince, and convert.

3. *Learned*

In addition, the Bible needs to be rediscovered as a Book to be learned. "As newborn babes," Peter wrote, "desire the sincere milk of the word, that ye may grow thereby" (1 Pet. 2:2, KJV).

The Bible is not simply an ornament to adorn our night stand. It is not just a good gift to give to a friend. It is a Book which is to be studied so that we can grow in our understanding of the faith.

In a discussion with his father, the son said, "Dad, I read the Bible often and memorize verses in Sunday School, but they never stick with me. I can't remember them more than a few weeks. So I guess it doesn't do me any good." The Father responded, "Son, get that wicker wastepaper basket, take it to the kitchen, and fill it up with water." The boy obeyed, but he discovered that the water ran out as fast as it went in. Finally, he took the basket back to his father. "I can't get any water to stay in," said the boy. "You're right. The basket cannot hold all the water, and your mind cannot hold all the verses you have memorized. But notice how much cleaner and fresher and brighter the basket is now that you've run the water through. That is what happens when all the verses of the Bible go through your mind. They may not stay there long enough for you to remember them, but the more you allow them to pass through your memory, the cleaner, the brighter, the fresher your mind will be."[12]

"Study to shew thyself approved unto God, a workman that needeth not to be ashamed" (2 Tim. 2:15, KJV). How we need to rediscover that truth.

4. *Lived*

Most of all, we need to rediscover the Bible as a Book to be lived. "Therefore," said Jesus, "whosoever heareth these sayings of mine, and doeth them, I will liken him unto a wise man, which built his house upon a rock" (Matt. 7:24, KJV).

One translator prefaced his 1734 edition of the Bible with this couplet: "Thy whole self apply to the text; The whole thing apply to thy self." If we would follow that advice, the power of God's Word would once more be discovered in our midst. Then, the kindling embers of renewal will blaze into the flame of revival in our land.

1 CHRONICLES

13. The Holiness of God

1 Chronicles 13:8-10

"Holy, Holy, Holy! Lord God Almighty!" If an ancient Israelite were to walk into one of our worship services today and hear us sing that hymn, he would feel right at home. For this was also one of his favorite themes as he worshiped God.

To the Israelite, holiness was not just an attribute of God. It was the essential reality of God to which all the other attributes related. God was preeminently the Holy One of Israel. One theologian concluded that "the word *holy* has become almost an epitome of the whole character of the God of Israel."

Nowhere is the holiness of God more evident than in the story recounted in our text. This awe-inspiring and perplexing story is imbedded in the narrative concerning the construction and dedication of the Temple. As several Hebrew men carried the ark of the Lord, Uzza put out his hand and touched the ark. Immediately, he died. Although some aspects of the story perplex us, the message is nevertheless clear. The experience is a declaration of the holiness of God.

The identity of God as the Holy One was the result of a long developmental process in Hebrew religious thought. Several aspects of God's holiness are evident in this process.

1. *Potency*

To say that God was holy was to say that he was transcendent. He was other than and apart from man. He was unique in his power.

This dimension of holiness is seen in the specific experiences related in the Bible. When the men of Bethshemesh were slain after looking into the ark of the covenant, the people cried,

"Who is able to stand before this holy Lord God?" (1 Sam. 6:20, KJV). When Uzzah touched the ark of God, he died (1 Chron. 13:8-10). When God gave Moses the Ten Commandments on Mount Sinai, the people were instructed not to come close to the mountain or gaze upon the place where God was lest they be destroyed (Ex. 19:21). When God appeared in the Temple to Isaiah, the walls shook and smoke filled the house (Isa. 6:4).

This element of holiness is also evident in the words that are related to holiness. Holiness and fear are closely related (Ps. 89:7). God is holy and terrible (Ps. 99:3). He is holy in his terrible works (Ex. 15:11; Ps. 66:3). Holiness and wrath are closely associated (Lev. 10:1-3). The imagery of fire and its substantives (smoke, heat, coals, light) are mentioned in relationship to holiness throughout the Old Testament (Isa. 6; Lev. 10:2; Ezek. 10:6-8).

God is a holy God! He is other than man. In this sense, holiness meant divine potency or power.

2. *Purity*

The idea of holiness also had a moral connotation. To say God was holy meant that he was pure. He was perfect in his righteousness. Thus, to come into his presence man must be holy or pure. "You shall be holy, for I the Lord your God am holy" (Lev. 19:2, RSV).

It is common to distinguish between the priestly and prophetic line of Hebrew thought at this point, concluding that the prophets were concerned with this moral dimension of God's holiness but the priests were not. A close study of the two lines will show convergence rather than contrast. To both prophet and priest, the Holy One was pure and to come into his presence, one must be pure.

Granted, the priestly and prophetic understanding of holiness was not always the same. To the priests, holiness was primarily ceremonial cleanness (Lev. 11:32; 13:6; 15:13). To the prophets, the purity which God exhibited and which man must emulate was primarily ethical cleanness (Amos 5:21,24;

Mic. 6:8). However, the ethical element was not altogether absent in the priestly message nor was the ceremonial element completely overlooked in the prophetic message.

The priests said that moral integrity was not enough to prepare one for the cultic encounter with God. One must also be ceremonially clean. The prophets said that ceremonial cleanness was not enough to prepare one for an encounter with God. One must also be ethically clean. Both agreed, however, that purity was necessary in order to come into the presence of God because he was pure.

To call God the Holy One not only referred to his potency and power. It also referred to his purity and perfection.

3. *Protection*

There is yet another dimension in the understanding of the holiness of God. The holiness of God came to be closely aligned with the idea of God's covenant with Israel. Yahweh was not simply the Holy One. He was the Holy One of Israel. Isaiah addressed God by this title thirty times. The title appears in Psalms 71:22; 78:41; 89:18, in Jeremiah 50:29; 51:5; and in Ezekiel 39:7.

To call God the Holy One of Israel meant that God keeps close to Israel and delivers his Chosen People according to his covenant with them. "As a soothing aroma," God said, "I shall accept you, when I bring you out from the peoples and gather you from the lands where you are scattered; and I shall prove Myself holy among you in the sight of the nations" (Ezek. 20:41, NASB).

To speak of God as holy referred not only to his potency and purity. It also proclaimed his protection of his covenant people.

4. *Conclusion*

When the ancient Israelite broke into a verse of "Holy, Holy, Holy!," he felt fear because of the potency of God. He recognized the need for cleansing because of the purity of God. Mainly, he felt gratitude because of the protection of God.

All these elements are beautifully blended into one of Israel's cultic songs:

The Lord reigns, let the peoples tremble;
He is enthroned above the cherubin, let the earth shake!
The Lord is great in Zion,
And He is exalted above all the peoples.
Let them praise Thy great and awesome name;
Holy is He.

And the strength of the King loves justice;
Thou hast established equity;
Thou hast executed justice and righteousness in Jacob.
Exalt the Lord our God.
And worship at His footstool;
Holy is He (Ps. 99:1-5, NASB).

2 CHRONICLES

14. Which Way, America?

2 Chronicles 7:14

After the Constitutional Convention, Benjamin Franklin made a haunting statement that comes again to each new generation of Americans: "We have given you a republic—if you can keep it."

The winds of dissent, discord, and deception that have blown across our land in the last decade have made the answer to that question uncertain. No one can honestly evaluate our country today without realizing that it is a dangerous time.

What is the heart of the crisis? Is it political? Economic? Sociological? No, it is a spiritual crisis. A recent survey revealed that the majority of twenty-one hundred young people interviewed said there is no living figure in America whom they admire and respect or with whom they can identify. It is clear that the real shortage in our day is not an energy shortage but a shortage in those personal attributes which lead to true greatness.

What is the prescription which will cure America's ills? To Israel, God suggested several qualities which must characterize any nation which wants to please Him.

1. *Responsibility*

In a day when the primary concern of most is with our rights, we must reawaken a concern for our responsibilities. And the responsibility must begin with God's people. When "My people who are called by My name" accept their responsibility, revival in America will begin.

It is so easy to hide behind the elusive "they." Look what "they" are doing. How can "they" be so bad? Why don't "they" do something about the problems? Our pretense is shattered, however, when we realize that the explosion of corruption in our land, the expansion of dishonesty which has spread to the highest offices in government, the erosion of morals which permeates our society is happening in an America with a church on almost every corner.

We can't blame our condition on the elusive "they." America is where it is today partly because we as God's people have not prayed long enough, have not loved deeply enough, have not given sacrificially enough, have not preached loudly enough, have not become involved diligently enough, have not witnessed passionately enough. Change will come only when we as God's people accept responsibility for what has happened.

2. *Humility*

We must then humble ourselves before Almighty God. How proud we have become of our freedom and how arrogant we are in our affluence. We take our freedom for granted, and are chafed by any attempt to limit our freedom. Our pride has blinded our eyes to the cost of our freedom. What we have, we have been given. And the cost was high. The blood of our ancestors is the price that was paid for it.

What happened to the men who signed the Declaration of Independence? Carter Braxton, a wealthy planter and trader, lost his ships to the British, sold his property to pay his debts, and died in rags. Thomas McKearn kept his family in hiding to protect them from the British. He served Congress without pay and ended up in poverty. Ellery, Clymer, Hall, Walton, Gwinnett, Heyward, Rutledge, and Middleton all had their homes looted by vandals and soldiers. John Hart was driven from his wife's bedside as she was dying. Their thirteen children fled for their lives. His fields and grist mill were destroyed. He returned home, after a year in caves and forests, to find his wife dead and his children vanished. Most of the others suffered similar fates.[13]

At such a great cost, our freedom has come to us. Instead of taking it for granted, we must humbly express our gratitude to God for this gift of liberty.

3. *Faith*

Having humbled ourselves before God, we must then pray and seek his face. We must return to faith as the foundation upon which our nation stands. How we need to hear again today the proclamation of Scripture, "Blessed is the nation whose God is the Lord" (Ps. 33:12, NASB).

During a dismal morning in World War I, David Lloyd George stood grimly before the members of the British cabinet. The seriousness of the situation was evident. The prime minister said, "Gentlemen, we are fighting with our backs to the wall. The only way out is up. Our only hope is God. Let us pray."

In our day when America is often too corrupt to be conquering and too comfortable to be courageous we need to proclaim to the world that the only way out is through faith and that our only hope is God.

4. *Integrity*

We must not only turn *to* God. We must also turn *from* our wicked ways. History has proven that the greatest enemy of any nation is not what attacks it from without but what corrodes it from within.

Bishop Sheen has pointed out that sixteen of the nineteen great civilizations that have passed away from the beginning of time have done so because of internal decay.

Alexis de Toqueville's statement is oft quoted but still a concise clarification of the place of integrity in American life. "America is great," said the Frenchman, "because America is good. If ever America ceases to be good, America will cease to be great." Then as now the word is "integrity."

5. *Conclusion*

Which way, America? God's way or the world's way? God's way will lead to his continued blessings upon us as a nation. The world's way will lead us eventually to the junk yard of nations. Which pathway will we take?

EZRA

15. What to Do with Your Religion

Ezra 7:10

It was a typical happening at a church youth camp. Billy had been invited by friends to attend. He went "just for the fun of it." However, at camp a serendipitous, spiritual something occurred. Billy met the Lord. He returned from youth camp that year a new person in Christ Jesus. Billy came by to see me the next week and asked a probing question: "I've been saved, Preacher. Now, what do I do?"

That's a question many people are asking. When you get religion, what do you do with it? We find some helpful suggestions in the description of Ezra in our text.

Ezra emerged as an important religious figure in Israel following the Babylonian captivity. When Judah was defeated by Babylon in 586 BC, the leaders of Judah were taken away to Babylon. Gradually, a shift of power occurred and Persia emerged as the preeminent power on the world scene. Cyrus, the Persian leader, reversed the practice of the Babylonians by allowing the captives to return to their homeland. His decree allowing the Jews to return to their homeland is recorded in Ezra 1. The first group returned to Judah in 536 BC under the leadership of Zerubbabel. Eighty years later, under Ezra, a second group returned.

Who was Ezra? A descendant of Aaron, Ezra was of the priestly line. He was an expert instructor in the Scriptures, a man of deep humility, godly purpose, and strong religious convictions. The description of him in our text reveals three things that Ezra did with his religion.

1. *He Studied It*

The desire to learn more about his faith is clearly exhibited in the opening statement of the verse: "For Ezra had set his heart to study the law of the Lord."

A doctor recently told me that a properly balanced diet is the crucial factor in good physical health, more important than physical environment, heredity, hygiene, or even exercise. Proper diet is the key to good physical health. That is also true spiritually. The most important ingredient in a growing Christian is a disciplined plan of study.

After one lesson, a lady told her husband that she wasn't going to take any more golf lessons. "Why not?" asked her husband. She responded, "I learned how to play yesterday."

You don't learn how to play golf in a day. Nor do you learn about God and his will for your life in a day. Elton Trueblood was closer to the truth when he said, "I hope to remain a student as long as I live."[14]

This study should begin with the Bible. Printed study guides are available from various sources. Or, you could read the Bible through, a chapter a day. Or, you could begin with a concentrated study of one book. Or, you could read each day until a special insight comes to you. Various plans should be tried. The key is to spend time in the Word of God.

This study should also include books and magazines which deal with themes of Christian living. Some of my keenest insights have come while reading the biographies of God's great saints.

Miles Standford, in his book on Christian growth, cites three reasons why believers fail to live their new life in Christ: lack of knowledge, misapplied knowledge, and unbalanced knowledge. All three inadequacies can be solved through study.[15]

We have too many hypodermic saints who live on a periodic injection of religious excitement. We need instead to have churches full of growing, maturing saints who are nourished by a regular, balanced diet of spiritual food.

2. *He Showed It*

Knowledge is never, however, an end in itself. Spiritual

knowledge must always find practical expression in our lives. We see this transition in Ezra. He not only studied his religion; he also showed it. Ezra had set his heart not only to study the law of the Lord but also "to practice it."

Albert Schweitzer once explained why he chose to go to Africa and bury his life there in service for Christ. "I came to Africa," he said, "because I wanted my life to be my argument. I didn't want my ideas to become an end in themselves."

The oft expressed question, "If you went on trial for being a Christian, would there be enough evidence to convict you?" is a timely question for every Christian of every generation. Is your life your argument? Do others know by watching you that you are a Christian?

3. *He Shared It*

Our text gives yet another insight into Ezra's religion. When the Bible says, "Ezra had set his heart . . . to teach His statutes and ordinances in Israel," we see that Ezra not only studied and showed his religion; he also shared it.

In June, 1981, the eyes of the world were focused on Frascati, Italy, where a little six-year-old boy had fallen into a deep well. A shaft was dug to free the boy, but then he fell deeper into the well. A midget was lowered two hundred feet into the shaft, but he was unable to free the boy. Ultimately, they gave up. In the newspaper article which reported the efforts to save the boy, the reporter told of the plaintive cry of the boy to his mother, relayed through a microphone lowered into the well. "Mamma, Mamma," he kept repeating, "When are you coming?"[16]

That is the cry of a lost and dying world. For man's guilt, we have the message of God's forgiveness. For man's confusion, we have the message of God's truth. For man's discontent, we have the message of God's fulfillment. From every direction comes the plaintive cry of the lost: "Christian, Christian, when are you coming?"

NEHEMIAH

16. When You Get Busy for God

Nehemiah 4:1-23

A Wyoming cattleman rode into a clearing out on the range and saw a wild bull attempting to gouge a cowboy who had fallen off his horse. Head down and nostrils snorting, the bull charged the man. The cowboy was saved by diving into a convenient recess in the ground. As soon as the bull plunged across the hole, the cowboy leaped out. The bull came back, madder than ever. Right before the bull reached him, the cowboy ducked back into the hole. Then, when the bull passed, he popped back out again. The cattleman watched this scenario several times. Finally, he shouted, "Hey, cowboy, why don't you just stay in the hole?" Leaping out again, the cowboy yelled, "There's a bear in that hole!"

That cowboy was caught between the proverbial "rock and a hard place." Whichever way he turned, there was trouble. That is an accurate parable of life for most of us. Trouble confronts us at every turn.

What is true of every area of life is also true in the realm of faith. Committing our lives to God does not remove us from the reality of problems in life. Trouble is still on the daily diet of every Christian. The lesson of the history of the church is that there is no commitment without conflict, no opportunity without opposition, no triumph without trouble. When you get busy for God, opposition will inevitably raise its head.

Nehemiah discovered that truth. Most historians believe that Nehemiah led a third group of Jews back to Judah after the Babylonian captivity. The date was about 444 BC. The task: to rebuild the walls of Jerusalem.

Who was Nehemiah? His name means "the comfort of

Jehovah." Born in the Exile period of Hebrew parents, his name indicates that he came from a deeply religious home. His purpose was certainly a worthy one: to reconstruct the walls of the city and to reconstruct the faith of the people. Yet, the moment he began, Nehemiah was confronted by opposition.

Nehemiah had opposition *from without*. Verses 1-6 indicate the scorn with which Nehemiah's enemies addressed him. "What are these feeble Jews doing?" the spectators asked (v. 2). "If a fox should jump on it, he would break their stone wall down!" the bystanders commented (v. 3). Verses 7-23 reveal that the scorn of his enemies soon developed into physical force. As the work of Nehemiah developed, the people in the land became angry and threatened to fight Nehemiah and his men. When we get busy for God, we too will often experience the scorn and physical force of the world.

Even more discouraging was the opposition *from within*. Nehemiah's most pressing problem was not from the enemies without but from his colleagues within. Verses 11-14 tell of the fear which gripped the people. As when the people of God stood paralyzed with fear at the threshold of the Promised Land, so God's people through the ages have often missed their golden opportunity because of fear. In Nehemiah 5:1-15 we see that greed also plagued the people of God. When the focus was turned from God to themselves, many of Nehemiah's contemporaries decided that the price they were having to pay was too great.

Both from without and from within, Nehemiah was confronted by obstacles as he sought to accomplish the work God called him to do. Nehemiah's story, however, was the story of overcoming obstacles. He was a success in the fullest meaning of the term. "So the wall was completed on the twenty-fifth of the month Elul, in fifty-two days" (Neh. 6:15, NASB). Despite the opposition, the work was done. The job was completed. In our text we discover the key ingredients that led to Nehemiah's success.

1. *Intercession*

When you get busy for God and opposition comes, the first ingredient that will lead to success is intercession. "But we prayed to our God," the Bible says (v. 9). Prayer was a key ingredient in Nehemiah's spiritual life (1:4). Nehemiah looked up before he launched out. He prayed before he proceeded. Intercession preceded interaction.

A visitor at Spurgeon's Tabernacle in London, England was being guided through the church. The guide asked the visitor if he would like to see the power plant of the church. Expecting to see the huge equipment which operated the building, the visitor followed the guide down into the basement. The guide opened the door to a room. Instead of being greeted by the noise of machinery, the visitor was confronted by over seven hundred people on their knees praying for the services!

The power plant in the life of every Christian is the devotional realm where he opens his life to the Heavenly Father through prayer.

2. *Initiative*

When you get busy for God and opposition comes, the second ingredient that will lead to success is initiative. Notice the practical tone of verse 9 (NASB): "But we prayed to our God, and because of them we set up a guard against them day and night." Intercession was not a substitute for initiative. Instead, it was a prelude to it, for the Bible says "the people had a mind to work" (v. 6).

One man asked George Muller to pray for him so that he would be able to get out of bed in the morning. Muller responded, "You get one leg out. Then, I'll pray for the other leg."

Our devotional life and practical life must always move together. They are like two sides to the coin, like two hands on a clock. The following statement has been attributed to various individuals. Whoever said it first, it nevertheless summarizes the key ingredients for Christian conquest: "I pray as if everything depended on God. Then I work as if everything depended on me." Intercession and initiative go together.

3. *Inspiration*

When you get busy for God and opposition comes, the third ingredient that will lead to success is inspiration. When confronted by the fear of the people, verse 14 says that Nehemiah arose and spoke to the people about the power of God ("remember the Lord who is great and awesome") and about the purpose of their work ("fight for your brothers, your sons, your daughters, your wives, and your houses"). When we are reminded of the purpose to which God has called us, and the power with which to accomplish that purpose, then we will be encouraged to move on toward the completion of our task.

There is powerful motivation in positive affirmation. Harold Warlick tells of a study in a California high school. At the beginning of the year, some teachers were told that certain students in their classes were potential geniuses. This information was supposedly the result of a series of tests. Actually, these students were not geniuses at all but were simply chosen at random. At the end of the school year, the results were shocking. The selected students scored far above their previous standings in class. Why? Because the teachers had been tricked into expecting, regarding, and treating them as if they were more capable than the other students. Positive affirmation resulted in positive accomplishment. They were inspired to greater heights by greater expectation.[17]

4. *Conclusion*

When you get busy for God, trouble is going to come. Expect it. As one old preacher put it, "When your cup runneth over, looketh out!" Through intercession, initiative, and inspiration, you can turn those stumbling blocks into stepping-stones. Obstacles can become opportunities for accomplishment. Trouble can be transformed into triumph.

ESTHER

17. The Odd Results of Trying to Get Even

Esther 7:8-10

In an ancient tale, a Greek athlete who lost a race was consequently filled with envy toward the winner. The crowd acclaimed the victor. A statue was constructed in his honor. Because of envy, the loser was determined to destroy the statue. Each night, under the cover of darkness, he chiseled away at the foundation of the statue. Finally, his work had been done and the statue fell. Right on top of the envious young man who died as a result of his own envy!

The high cost of getting even is also seen in a poignant tale in the Book of Esther. Esther is a uniquely beautiful book which has been ambivalently evaluated over the centuries. Martin Luther desired to dispose of it because "it Judaized too much." On the other hand, Maimonides, the medievel Jewish theologian, rated it with the Torah as the most holy of the Scriptures.

The agenda of the Book of Esther is to describe what happened to the Jews who were not a part of the remnant returning with Zerubbabel to Judah in 536 BC. Esther is the star of the story, but the real drama is the interplay between Mordecai (the good guy) and Haman (the bad guy). Read chapters 5 and 6 to get the background for the final ploy. Haman, setting himself up for the honor of the king, built a gallows upon which he thought Mordecai would be executed. By an ironic twist of fate, the king learned of a reason to honor Mordecai and at the same time discovered the deplorable deception of Haman. Haman's perverted plan for preeminence backfired, and his eventual fate was determined: "So they hanged

Haman on the gallows which he had prepared for Mordecai" (7:10, NASB).

This is more than a story from an ancient age. It is a parable of life in every age. And it clearly reveals the odd results of trying to get even. This story focuses the spotlight on envy, the marauder of the soul.

1. *The Cause*

From what source does envy spring up in the human heart?

One source of envy is *desire*. Envy emerges when we see something that another person possesses, and we want it for ourselves. It may be possessions or position or prominence. In the case of Haman, it was Mordecai's submission that he desired. By his refusal to bow to Haman, Mordecai deprived Haman of the one thing he most desired. The Bible says, "And when Haman saw that Mordecai bowed not, nor did him reverence, then was Haman full of wrath" (3:5, KJV).

Another source of envy is *defeat*. Envy usually evolves out of failure. Defeated ourselves, we become envious of others who have succeeded. Haman saw Mordecai's refusal to submit to him as a personal defeat. The result was envy.

A clearer example is the rift between Saul and David (1 Sam. 18:6-12). Saul felt his power slipping while at the same time David's star of fame was soaring. Consequently, Saul envied the young competitor who was accomplishing success at the expense of Saul's defeat.

Desire and defeat are the seeds which blossom forth into envy. Both are clearly demonstrated in Haman.

2. *The Curse*

What does envy do to us? Why is it forbidden by Paul (Gal. 5:26)? Why did the writer of Proverbs declare, "Who is able to stand before envy (Prov. 27:4, KJV)?"

Envy *distorts* our thinking. The passion of envy is so powerful that it becomes the dominant force before which all other thoughts become subservient. When Haman heard of the feast of Esther and anticipated great honor to be bestowed on him, he nevertheless said, "Yet all this availeth me nothing, so long as I see Mordecai the Jew sitting at the king's gate" (5:13, KJV). He could think of only one thing. He wanted to get even with Mordecai.

Envy *disturbs* our soul. Joy and jealousy are incompatible emotions. Study the portrait of Haman in chapters 3 through 6, and you will discover that his envy had taken the joy and contentment out of his life.

Envy *disrupts* our relationship with God. This is implied but not clearly stated in Haman's experience. Envy is a sin. And the Scriptures clearly declare that sin harbored in our hearts creates a barrier between us and God (Isa. 59:2).

Envy eventually *destroys* our lives. This was the ultimate outcome in the life of Haman. He envied Mordecai and wanted to destroy him. Instead, "they hanged Haman on the gallows which he had prepared for Mordecai" (7:10, NASB).

3. *The Cure*

So what can we do about it? When envy emerges, how can we deal with it?

The first step is to *recognize* it. When we go to the doctor, the first step is diagnosis. Until the problem is pinpointed, the proper cure cannot be prescribed. Watch out for envy.

The second step is to *release* it. Envy is a sin. Don't hide it. Don't hold on to it. Confess it. The promise of God's forgiveness hinges on our willingness to confess our sins to him (1 John 1:9).

The third step is to *rely* on the Holy Spirit. We cannot overcome envy on our own, nor do we need to. The power of God is available to every believer. Reliance upon his power will enable us to be "more than conquerors through him that loved us" (Rom. 8:37, KJV).

The fourth step is to *realize* our own self-worth. The Bible says that each of us as Christians has been endowed with a spiritual gift, and each of us has been ordained for a special goal. Translated into simple terms, that means that each of us is somebody special to God! When we accept that truth, envy will be evicted from our lives.

JOB

18. The Arm of God

Job 40:9

What a remarkable turnabout we see in the life of Job. The American dream is the story of the ascent from rags to riches. Job reversed the process, for his was the story of the descent from riches to rags. The first five verses in the Book of Job picture him as a man spotless in character, shrewd in his business skill, serious in his religious commitment, and singularly blessed in his family. He was, the Bible says, "the greatest of all the men in the east" (1:3). Then, tragedy struck. Job's family was destroyed. His wealth was taken away. His health was affected. His reputation and religious commitment were called into question. Job was in trouble.

A major section of the book describes the response of Job's friends to his trouble. Rather than bringing relief, these three friends intensified the feeling within Job that he had been mistreated by life. In the end, Job laid his case before God. Job accused God of injustice. He accused God of indifference. He accused God of incompetence. In the midst of his darkness, Job shouted, "Why has this happened to me?"

God responded to Job, not with an answer but with a question. God did not explain his action. He did not defend his action. Rather, he asked a question of penetrating importance: "Do you have an arm like God?" (Job 40:9, NASB).

Over forty times in the Old Testament, reference is made to the arm of God. It is called a mighty arm (Ps. 89:13), a holy arm (Isa. 52:10), a glorious arm (Isa. 63:12), an outstretched arm (Ex. 6:6), and an everlasting arm (Deut. 33:27). The arm of God is a common symbol in the Old Testament.

But what does it mean? What did God mean when he confronted Job with the question about his arm? The arm was man's chief member for putting into effect the dictates of his will. It was a symbol of a man's power or strength. The arm of God, therefore, refers to the strength or power of God.

This, then, is the picture of our text. Job cried out to God in his despair, and God responded, not with an answer to his questions, not with an explanation for his suffering, but with the ringing reminder of his power and his glory and his majesty. "Does anyone," God asked, "have an arm like mine?"

We need that message today. Our greatest need is not to have all of our questions answered, for many of our questions are meaningless. Our greatest need is not to have our suffering explained, for even if God would do that we with our finite minds could not comprehend it. Our greatest need, in the midst of the darkness of our day, is the reminder of the sufficiency of the power and might of God. We need to be reminded that the God whom we worship and serve is not weak and incompetent. He is a God who is able. He is able to bring low the proud, to lift up the discouraged, to defeat the evil forces of life, to meet every need of our lives. We need to be reminded that no one has an arm like God.

1. *Sustains the World*

Who has an arm like God? No one, for with his mighty arm, God sustains the world. God passed before Job a panoramic view of the universe, the manifold mysteries of the heavens and the earth (38:1-38), and the equally mysterious and incomprehensible world of living creatures (38:39 to 39:30). Then, God asked Job if he was equal either to the creation or the government of what he saw. The only answer Job could give was, "No."

The ability to send capsules catapulting through space at a speed of thousands of miles per hour is a significant accomplishment of our day. However, lest we think too highly of this accomplishment, let us remember that our man-made instruments are barely moving in comparison to the movements of the God-created and God-sustained universe.

Take the earth, for instance. If you began reading this book and have read to this chapter in one sitting, from the time you began our earth has been hurtled through space a distance of about 50,000 miles. At a speed of 1,600,000 miles per day, our earth travels around the sun. At the same time, the earth is rotating on its axis. Yet, all of this movement occurs in such a way that we are not slung off of its surface!

Like Job, we often cry out in anguish, "God, do something or say something spectacular to let us know that you are in charge. Just let a star fall or cause the earth to stop for a moment or create before our eyes something fantastic. Do something to let us see your power." All the while, God is showing us he is in charge, he is demonstrating his power, by keeping the stars up in the sky and by keeping the earth hurtling through space in its predetermined pattern.

Who has an arm like God? No one, for with his mighty arm God sustains the world.

2. *Shows the Way*

Who has an arm like God? No one, for with his mighty arm, God shows the way. The incredible message of the Bible is that the God who sustains the world in all of its majesty is a God who becomes involved in the lives of his people, and he is able to direct our paths.

This is the great truth with which God confronted Job. God did not erase the hurt that Job felt. He did not explain the tragedy. He did not directly answer the charges. What God did was to plant within the mind of Job that exhilarating reminder that in the processes of life, God is exerting his daily leadership in the lives of his people.

How does God guide us? Three road signs point the way for us: the commands of Scripture, the communication of the Spirit, and the combination of situations.

About the Scriptures, Jesus said: "If you abide in My word, then you are truly disciples of Mine; and you shall know the truth, and the truth shall make you free" (John 8:31*b*-32, NASB).

About the Spirit, Jesus said, "But when He, the Spirit of

truth, comes, He will guide you into all the truth; for He will not speak on His own initiative, but whatever He hears, He will speak; and He will disclose to you what is to come" (John 16:13, NASB).

The guidance of God in our situations is best seen not in a particular verse but in Acts 16 where we see God opening and closing doors for Paul until Luke could say, "We sought to go into Macedonia, concluding that God had called us to preach the gospel to them" (Acts 16:10, NASB).

Who has an arm like God's? No one, for with his mighty arm he shows the way.

3. *Strengthens the Weak*

Who has an arm like God's? No one, for with his mighty arm he strengthens the weak. The ultimate result of Job's encounter with God is that Job experienced strength which enabled him to make it through the darkness.

The good news of God's Word is that, with his mighty arm, God is able to give you the strength to make it through.

God might come to you in the whirlwind like he did to Job or in the still small voice like he did to Elijah. He might come to you in the blinding appearance on some Damascus road like he did to Paul or in the solemn stillness of the night like he did to Samuel. He might come to you in the solitude of the wilderness like he did to Moses, or in the midst of a thronging, worshiping multitude like he did to Isaiah in the temple. God will burst into your life and with his mighty arm, he will give to you the interior resources to face every difficulty of your life.

Several years ago a group of tourists was going through the Carlsbad Caverns in New Mexico. In the group was a father, a mother, and two children. At the deepest point of the cavern, the guide suddenly turned off the light to dramatize how utterly dark and silent it is so far below the surface of the earth. Out of the darkness came two sounds. The first was the startled cry of the little girl who had been surprised by the darkness. The other, seconds later, was the reassuring voice of her older brother saying, "Don't cry, little sister, there is somebody here who knows how to turn on the lights."

God has the whole world in his hands. He guides the pathway of those who will listen to his voice. And he can transform bleak and desolate valleys of darkness into sunlit paths of joy. No one, but no one, has an arm like God!

PSALMS

19. The Problem of Suffering

Psalm 73

I still remember when the ravages of Vietnam became real to me. A young man in the community where I pastored, still a teenager, was wounded in action in the war. After several months of recuperation in hospitals in the Philippines and Japan, David was transferred to a hospital in San Antonio, Texas. I drove down to visit him. I found him in a large ward where a hundred beds were filled with men with a hundred different kinds of broken and wounded bodies. As I walked into the room I was confronted by a young man in a wheelchair with a handsome face and a wealth of untapped potential. But he had no arms and no legs. For the first time in my life I came face to face with the enigma of human suffering.

This problem of human suffering is addressed by the psalmist in our text. What compounded the problem for him was the observation that the righteous seemed to suffer more than the unrighteous. The wicked cursed God; yet they seemed to be basking in prosperity. The psalmist tried to live the righteous life and do what God wanted him to do; yet he confessed that it was as if the very foundation of his life had been swept out from under him (v. 2).

Because all of us have been in the psalmist's shoes, it is important to hear what he had to say about the problem of suffering. The question he addresses is not "Why does suffering come?" but rather, "What does God do in the midst of the suffering?" He is not giving an explanation of suffering. Instead, he is describing the resources available to us in the midst of suffering. The psalmist discovered three things that he could count on God for.

1. *His Presence*

God does not promise to remove suffering from our lives, but he does promise his presence in the midst of our suffering. The psalmist found that when the foundation of his life shook, God took hold of his right hand (v. 23).

The message of God which was unforgettably proclaimed to the world on Calvary was proclaimed repeated in the Old Testament as well. Often we think of God as merely a spectator, dealing out pain and suffering to see how men will react. A glimpse at the cross, however, will remind us that the sufferer hanging there is not just another martyr dying for his faith but the incarnate God dying for the world. Then we will realize that God is not outside the tears and tragedy of life. He is in it with us.

The lesson of Shadrach, Meshach, and Abednego is that whenever God puts his children in the fire or allows them to be put in the fire, he is going to be in the fire with them (Dan. 3). That is the truth the psalmist discovered. God will be with us in our suffering.

An old Scotsman who was very ill was visited by his minister. As the pastor sat down by the bed, he noticed another chair by the other side of the bed. The pastor asked him about the chair and the old saint replied, "Years ago I found it difficult to pray. One day I discussed this problem with my pastor. He told me not to worry about kneeling down. 'Just sit down,' he told me, 'put a chair opposite you, and imagine Jesus in it, and talk to him as you would to a friend.' " The old Scotsman added, "I've been doing it ever since."

A short while later the daughter of the sick man called to tell the minister her father had died. She said, "I laid down for an hour or two because he seemed to be sleeping comfortably. When I went back to check on him, he was dead. He had not moved since I left him, except that his hand was on the empty chair at the side of the bed."[18]

In the midst of suffering, God is there. And you can put your hand in his.

2. *His Power*

There is more. In verse 24 the psalmist indicated that God also promised his power. God will not only be with us in the suffering; he will also guide us through it and enable us to win over it. When God comes to us, he comes with power.

It was the power of God's presence that enabled Joseph to win victory over his suffering in the dungeon, that enabled Daniel to win victory over his suffering in the lion's den, that enabled Simon Peter to win victory in his dark night of the soul after he denied Jesus, that enabled Paul to win victory over his thorn in the flesh.

In the midst of our suffering God promises to come with such power that he will enable us to be, in the words of Paul, "more than conquerors through him who loved us" (Rom. 8:37, RSV).

Christian Reger was thrown into the terror of Dachau. Prisoners were allowed one letter a month, and after the first month he was given a letter from his wife. The letter was censored, but a biblical reference was left in: Acts 4:26-29. In this speech by Peter and John after being released from prison, these first disciples said, "Now, Lord, consider their threats and enable your servants to speak your word with great boldness" (NIV).

That afternoon Christian had to face interrogators, one of the most terrifying experiences in the camp. He could be beaten, and even killed. He approached the interrogation room with fear and trembling. When the door opened, a fellow minister came out whom Christian had never met. Without changing his expression, this man slipped something into Christian's pocket, and walked away. Then Christian was ushered into the interrogation room. The interrogation was surprisingly mild, and soon Christian was back in the barracks. When he had calmed down, he pulled out a matchbox which the minister had slipped into his pocket. Inside the matchbox was a folded slip of paper. Neatly printed on the paper was this reference: Acts 4:26-29.

This may seem small to us, but to Christian it was a message from God. He was convinced that God had arranged the event as a demonstration that He was still alive, still able to strengthen, still worthy of trust. It was a sign that God's power was sufficient, even at Dachau.[19]

3. *His Perspective*

Look again at verse 24 and you will discover yet another promise of God. The psalmist realized that someday the accounts will be balanced, and that our suffering will be eclipsed by the glory of God's eternal presence. In worship, the psalmist was given the perspective of God. The pleasure of the wicked was only temporary. It would someday be brought to an end. Likewise, his suffering was only temporary, for afterward he believed that God would receive him to glory.

Paul said it like this: "For I consider that the sufferings of this present time are not worthy to be compared with the glory that is to be revealed to us" (Rom. 8:18).

George Matheson, the blind poet and preacher, is remembered for his famous hymn, "O Love That Wilt Not Let Me Go." Equally as moving is a lesser known prayer which goes like this: "My God, I have never thanked Thee for my thorns. I have thanked Thee a thousand times for my roses, but not once for my thorns . . . teach me the value of my thorns. Show me that I have climbed to Thee by the path of pain. Show me that my tears have made my rainbow."[20]

In worship, the psalmist discovered the presence, power, and perspective of God which come in the midst of suffering. And God brought a rainbow of hope out of his tears.

PROVERBS

20. What God Hates

Proverbs 6:16-19

The words *hate* and *God* do not seem to go together. Yet, the writer of Proverbs clearly declares that God hates something. What is it? Our initial instinct would be to nominate the terrible two: murder and adultery. Others would suggest drunkenness or debauchery. Not so, according to the writer of Proverbs. What God hates is the misuse of the parts of the body God intended to be blessings.

No part of God's creation is any more remarkable than the creature called man. Packed under the skin of man are some 263 bones tied together with more than 500 muscles. All of this is temperature controlled with the most wonderful air-conditioning system in the world. The body is operated by one central muscle 6 inches by 4 inches which beats nearly 2½ billion times in 70 years, and pumps more than 7 tons of blood daily through more than 100,000 miles of blood vessels. This heart is the energy center of the body. The intellectual and motivational center of the body is a remarkable computer the size of a soft, squishy grapefruit that we call the brain. Imagine a computer with ten billion transistors and ten trillion wires which can add up grocery bills and write songs and appreciate art and dream of dragons and fall in love! It is no wonder the psalmist cried, "I will give thanks to Thee, for I am fearfully and wonderfully made" (Ps. 139:14).

Why did God give us this remarkable body? He gave us our eyes to see his light, our tongue to proclaim his truth, our heart to feel his compassion, our hands to hold out his blessings, our feet to follow his way. But the writer of Proverbs tells us that God hates our misuse of these sensational tools.

1. *Misuse of Our Eyes*

What does God hate? He hates "haughty eyes" (v. 17). The eyes are the windows which determine what comes into the brain, for 300,000 telephone lines connect the eyes to the brain and immediately communicate images to the brain. The eyes can flood the soul with light, or they can contaminate the soul with darkness. So said Jesus in the Sermon on the Mount, "The lamp of the body is the eye; if therefore your eye is clear, your whole body will be full of light. But if your eye is bad, your whole body will be full of darkness. If therefore the light that is in you is darkness, how great is the darkness!" (Matt. 6:22-23, NASB).

2. *Misuse of Our Tongues*

What does God hate? He hates "a lying tongue" (v. 17), and "a false witness who utters lies" (v. 19). The Bible repeatedly declares that our tongue is to be used to speak the truth. We are to walk before God in truth (1 Kings 2:4), love truth (Zech. 8:19), rejoice in the truth (1 Cor. 13:6), meditate upon the truth (Phil. 4:8), and speak to one another in truth (Eph. 4:25).

Honesty is the best policy for the Christian, not only because God commands it but also because dishonesty has a way of backfiring. A stingy soul needed to send a birthday present to a friend, but he didn't want to spend much money. He noticed in the store a broken vase that the owner was about to throw away. He bought it for almost nothing and asked the store to mail it to his friend. He knew, of course, that the friend would think the expensive gift had been broken by the postal service enroute. A week later the stingy giver received a brief note: "Many thanks for the lovely vase. It was nice of you to have each broken piece wrapped separately!"

3. *Misuse of Our Hands*

What does God hate? He hates "hands that shed innocent blood" (v. 17). A noted hand analyst from New York asserts that the secrets of our personality are revealed by our fingernails. The size and shape of each fingernail reveals something about the personality characteristics of a person. I am not sure about that. This much, however, is certain. We reveal our personality by what we do with our hands.

Several years ago a sixteen-year-old girl was critically ill in one of the charity hospitals of London. She was the eldest child of a large and extremely poor family. Because her mother died while giving birth to the last baby, this girl had become the mother of the home. She had literally worked herself to death. A visitor from one of the churches entered her room and began to quiz her: "Are you a member of the church? Have you been baptized? Did you ever go to Sunday School? Do you know the Ten Commandments?" On and on the lady went, and to each question the girl answered no. Finally, the woman asked, "What will you do when you die and have to tell God that?" The young lady, who had early in her life made her commitment to God and who had lived out that commitment to God in service to her family, laid two thin, work-stained hands on the bedspread and looked at the woman with dark eyes too full of peace to be disturbed. Then she very quietly said, "I shall show him my hands."

Praying, busy, compassionate, pure hands dedicated in service to God are a blessing to him. Hands which "shed innocent blood" God hates.

4. *Misuse of Our Hearts*

What does God hate? He hates "a heart that devises wicked plans" (v. 18). In biblical anatomy, the heart was the center of emotions. It was the emoting, thinking, deliberating center of the personality. It held the place in biblical anatomy that the mind holds in our anatomical understanding today.

The most neglected part of the body today is the brain, the mental center of our being. Experts suggest that most people in their lifetime use only about 10 to 20 percent of their brain power. Neglect of our brain power is not nearly as tragic as directing our mental powers to perpetrate evil rather than good.

What is the solution? Paul suggests a workable mental hygiene program in his letter to the Philippian Christians (Phil. 4:8). By concentrating our attention on the truth as opposed to falsehood, on the serious as opposed to the frivolous, on the right as opposed to the convenient, on the clean as opposed to the dirty, on the loving as opposed to the discordant, on the positive as opposed to the negative, then we too can have the mind of Christ (Phil. 2:5).

5. *Misuse of our Feet*

What does God hate? He hates "feet that run rapidly to evil" (v. 18). The average person takes 18,000 steps a day and walks about 65,000 miles during a lifetime. More important than how far we travel is where we travel.

Two admonitions are given in the Scriptures concerning our feet. With our feet, we are to follow Christ (Matt. 8:22). With our feet, we are to flee from evil (1 Cor. 6:18).

The man who "does not walk in the counsel of the wicked" is considered to be blessed before God (Ps. 1:1, NASB). When we run rapidly to evil, God hates it.

6. *Conclusion*

William Arthur Ward has said, "We were created to expand our consciousness through prayer, to extend our hands in service, to express our thanks with joy, to expend our energies with wisdom, and to exemplify our love by deeds."[21] When we do, we are a blessing to God. What God hates is the misuse of this remarkable body which he has given us.

ECCLESIASTES

21. Two Are Better than One

Ecclesiastes 4:9-12

Recent surveys have revealed a growing dissatisfaction with marriage. Several explanations are given to explain this trend. Some say it reflects a greater openness in discussing our problems today than in the past. Circumstances have not changed, just the conversation about the circumstances.

Others relate the problem to the narcissistic bent of our age when everyone seems to be more concerned with self-fulfillment than with fidelity. Others suggest that higher expectations with which a person enters marriage in our time lead to greater dissatisfaction. However you explain it, it is evident that something serious is happening between "here comes the bride" and "here comes the judge." Marriage, which is meant to be life's most glorious relationship, often deteriorates into a daily dilemma of debts, dishes, drudgery, doubts, and diapers. Marriage loses its spice!

What are we to do? Some opt for divorce. A sensitive teacher spoke to a boy in her class whose parents had just divorced. She said, "I know you have a problem at home and I want to help." The boy responded, "We had a problem at home, but we divorced him." Such is the out for many. Others just fight it out to the bitter end. One husband said to his wife, "We've been married for six weeks and we haven't agreed on anything yet." She responded, "It's been seven weeks." And there they went again!

Is marriage obsolete? Is marital happiness an impossible dream in our day? No, because it is God's plan. The writer of Ecclesiastes saw the value of God's plan when he wrote, "Two are better than one because they have a good return for their labor" (v. 9, NASB). Why are two better than one? What is the value of marriage for us today? Notice three benefits the writer of Ecclesiastes mentioned.

1. *Support*

Two are better than one because you have someone to support you, and someone you can support. The writer of Ecclesiastes said in verse 10: "For if either of them falls, the one will lift up his companion."

Someone has suggested that love means making your problems my problems for as long as we live. That's the way it is in marriage at its best. We never tire of helping one another, assisting one another, encouraging one another, and affirming one another.

Ours is a critical age. Opposition and criticism are a part of our daily diet. One study showed that in the daily routine of ordinary businessmen, 67 percent of the verbal input of their lives was critical. In our dog-eat-dog, critical, competitive world, we need someone who will love us and support us and encourage us. One husband said, "My wife makes me feel good about myself with a pat high on the ego." We all need that. The home is where it should be found.

Often, however, the critical spirit of our day creeps into our homes as well. Rather than supporting each other, we often pick each other apart. One lady told her pastor that the man who had been the apple of her eye was now the core of her discontent!

How can we maintain the home as a support system for each other? One of the best prescriptions is found in the ancient prayer by Francis of Assisi (1182-1226). "Lord, make me an instrument of Thy peace; where there is hatred, let me sow love; where there is injury, pardon; where there is doubt, faith; where there is despair, hope; where there is darkness, light; where there is sadness, joy. O divine Master, grant that I may not so much seek to be consoled as to console, to be understood as to understand, to be loved as to love."

With that attitude motivating us, we will once more begin to support each other in the home, and we will rediscover why two are better than one.

2. *Share*

Two can be better than one because we have someone to share with. Verse 11 says, "Furthermore, if two lie down together they keep warm, but how can one be warm alone?"

The basic purpose of marraige according to Genesis 2:24 (NASB) is intimacy. The Bible says, "For this cause a man shall leave his father and his mother, and shall cleave to his wife; and they shall become one flesh." The word "cleave" means to be glued together and suggests the closest, strongest, most intimate kind of relationship. The word depicts a total sharing of two people with each other.

Do you remember when you first fell in love? Remember how you could talk for hours, about anything and everything? About nothing? And when you didn't have anything to say, you just sat and held hands? Remember how you would spend an evening together and then as soon as you got home, pick up the phone and call your honey so you could talk some more? Remember how, when you had a decision to make, you would not deal with it until you talked about it with your true love? Remember when something exciting would happen, and you would just about bust before you could tell your true love about it? Remember how you shared everything with each other? That is the purpose of marriage, to experience the joy of intimacy.

An older couple was driving down the street. They passed a couple of newlyweds in a car. The newlyweds were practically sitting in each others' laps. The older lady said, "Isn't that romantic. Why don't we do that anymore?" The husband replied, "I haven't moved!"

The problem with marriage today is not that we share too much but that we share too little, not that we are too close but that we have gradually moved apart. When we once more begin to share everything with each other, then we will rediscover why two are better than one.

3. *Strengthen*

Two are better than one because there is strength in numbers. Verse 12 (NASB) says, "And if one can overpower him who is alone, two can resist him."

David Mace has said, "The most satisfying kind of marriage is that in which the couple think of their intimate life together as a secluded wall garden where no one else ever comes—a little private kingdom."[22] Unreserved fidelity to each other provides a power base from which we can face all that life has to offer.

Marriage provides strength for making the *decisions* of life. One single recently confided, "I just wish I had someone to talk to when I had to make a decision." Two are better than one.

Marriage provides strength for facing the *dilemmas* of life. A lady in the hospital recently told me, "My husband has been a real jewel. I couldn't have made it without him." Two are better than one.

Marriage provides strength for avoiding the *deception* of life. A politician stood before a large crowd and said, "I am glad to see such a dense crowd of people gathered here today," to which one man responded, "We ain't as dense as he thinks." The truth is, most of us are pretty dense. So often our perception is limited, our objectivity is shaded. We need someone to help us see the matter from a different viewpoint. Two are better than one.

Marriage provides strength for fulfilling the *demands* of life. Have you ever watched tag team wrestling? One man will be about to go under. Then, he reaches out and touches his partner who comes rushing in to the rescue. That's a beautiful picture of marriage, of partners who are ready to rush in at any given moment to rescue the other person. Two are better than one.

The statement of the single woman who declared, "All men are selfish, brutal, and inconsiderate, and I wish I could find one" is explained by the simple truth of our text: two can be better than one.

THE SONG OF SOLOMON

22. And This Is Love

The Song of Solomon 2:2-4 (TEV)

What is love? One man defined it as a four-letter word consisting of two consonants, L and V, two vowels, O and E, and two fools, you and me! Another man said that if life is one crazy thing after another, love must be two crazy things after each other. A cartoon depicts two people, a man and a woman, on a dogsled in Alaska. The man said to the woman, "I'd drive my dog team one hundred miles to say 'I Love You' " to which the woman responded, "That's a lot of mush!"

Is that what love is? Two fools, you and me; two crazy things after each other; a lot of mush? What is love? One of the most beautiful biblical answers to that question is the Song of Solomon.

Much controversy has swirled around this unique Old Testament book. Some see the story to be an allegory about the love of God for his Chosen People. Others feel the story is an actual depiction of human love between a man and a woman. I believe that it is both. The Song of Solomon is first of all a collection of love songs describing the love of a man for a woman. This human love story becomes an allegory describing God's love for his people.

The inclusion of the book in the Old Testament canon demonstrates the sanctity of human love and the sacredness of the relationship between a man and a woman. And it provides some insight into the key ingredients of genuine love.

In true love, there is:

1. *Appeal*

In verse 2 the man, addressing the woman, declared, "Like a lily among thorns is my darling among women" (TEV). She had an unusual appeal to him. Psychologists use the term "halo effect" to speak of this phenomenon. According to the halo effect, your general feeling about someone else influences your evaluation of his or her specific attributes or abilities. If you love a woman, you will probably think that she is smarter and better looking than you would if you didn't like her. If you love a man, you will probably believe him to be more intelligent and more handsome than if you didn't like him. In real love, the other person has a unique appeal to you.

Judith Viorst, writing in *Redbook*, humorously illustrated this quality of love. She defined the difference between infatuation and love like this: "Infatuation is when you think he's as sexy as Robert Redford, as smart as Henry Kissinger, as noble as Ralph Nader, as funny as Woody Allen, and as athletic as Jimmy Connors. Love is when you realize he's as sexy as Woody Allen, as smart as Jimmy Connors, as funny as Ralph Nader, as athletic as Henry Kissinger, and nothing like Robert Redford—but you'll take him anyway."[23]

When you love someone you see the best in that person. There is an appeal about that person which causes you to say, "Like a lily among the thorns is my darling among women."

In real love, there is:

2. *Attention*

The woman in the Song of Solomon said of her sweetheart: "Like an apple tree among the trees of the forest, so is my dearest compared to other men. I love to sit in its shadow" (v. 3, TEV). When you love someone you want to be with him/her, and your thoughts are often tuned in to that person. As one modern sage put it, "She loves him if, when she's not thinking about him, she's thinking about him."

A popular comedian once told the story of a young man in Java who spotted a beautiful young lady walking down the road. He fell in right behind her and followed her for over a mile. Finally, the young lady wheeled around and demanded, "Why do you dog my footsteps?" With fervent emotion he replied, "Because you are the loveliest thing I have ever seen, and I have fallen madly in love with you at first sight. Please be mine." The young lady responded, "You only have to look behind you and you will see my younger sister who is ten times more beautiful than I." He turned quickly to see as ugly a girl as he had ever seen. "What a mockery!" he said to the beautiful maiden, "You lied to me!" "So did you," she replied. "If you were so madly in love with me, why did you turn around?"

When love is real, you won't turn around. Your attention will be on the one you love, for you will enjoy sitting in the shadow of her presence.

In real love, there is:

3. *Action*

The lover in the Song of Solomon did not simply talk about his concern. He showed it. For his sweetheart declared of him, "He brought me to his banquet hall and raised the banner of love over me" (v. 4, TEV). Genuine love not only thinks about the other person. Love acts out that concern in providing for the person's needs.

This is the chief contrast between real love and reel love, between genuine love and the Hollywood version. Reel love asks, "What can I get?" Real love asks, "What can I give?" Reel love asks, "How does it feel?" Real love asks, "What can I do?"

What is love? Three plain evidences of love are appeal, attention, and action. And that's no mush!

ISAIAH

23. When God Calls

Isaiah 6:1-8

As a high school senior, I began to sense God working in my life in a special way. From childhood, my plans were to become a doctor. In my senior year, I sensed a new direction emerging before me. Each Sunday the feeling was intensified. A growing desire to preach captured my imagination. Hours of careful counsel from my pastor helped me decide finally to follow a life in the ministry. One statement my pastor made has stuck with me since that time: "The most important thing is not if you are capable but if you have been called."

Called of God! That sounds ominous. Yet, at the heart of our faith is the conviction that God does indeed call some to preach the gospel. According to his purpose, the Holy Spirit gives gifts to the children of God, plans a ministry in which those gifts can be utilized, and then confronts us with the challenge to use them.

Isaiah, too, felt the call of God. His dramatic call and his daring response to it are recorded in the sixth chapter of his prophecy. Notice several things about the call of God.

1. *Preparation*

We see first the preparation for God's call. Verse 1 tells us that Isaiah was in the Temple when he heard the call of God. Isaiah's world was falling apart. The death of Uzziah was not just the death of another man. His death marked the end of an era. Uncertainty resulted. What a shattering time this was for young Isaiah. Yet, in those dark moments of despair, Isaiah did what he had always done. He came before God in prayer and worship. In the communion of his soul with God, he had his ears opened to the voice of God.

Many young people share with me that they do not know what God wants them to do. They read about an experience like Isaiah's and reply, "That has never happened to me. I have never heard God speak to me." Perhaps the reason they do not discern the will of God is that they are not spiritually prepared to receive it. They do not receive God's call because they are not within calling distance.

G. Campbell Morgan once wrote a minister asking him to come deliver an address at a Sunday School anniversary service. Receiving no answer for two weeks, Morgan wrote again, thinking the letter had been lost in the mail. The preacher responded to Morgan's second letter by saying, "Yes, I received the first letter. I have not yet answered because I am waiting on the Lord in prayer to know whether I should accept or not." Morgan wrote the minister back and canceled the invitation with the rejoinder: "I don't want as our anniversary preacher a man who lives so far away from the Lord that he has to wait two weeks to hear His voice!"[24]

In contrast, notice what happened to Isaiah. If this was a regular worship service, Isaiah was not alone in the Temple. Crowding around him from every side were the hundreds who had come to worship. Isaiah was not alone in the Temple that day, but he alone saw the vision. He alone beheld the glory. He alone heard God's call. Why? Because he lived close to God. His heart had already been tuned in with God's through a long period of prayer, study, and devotion. He was prepared to hear God's call.

2. *Pervasiveness*

We also see the pervasiveness of God's call. Isaiah says that he saw the Lord high and lifted up, and that the train of the Lord's robe filled the Temple (v. 1). The foundation of the Temple trembled as the voice of God spoke, and the house was filled with smoke (v. 4). Isaiah said that it was as if the very glory of God filled the Temple. In that moment, Isaiah experienced an awareness of God completely surrounding him. God was everywhere. God's presence was a pervasive presence from which he could not escape. From every direction came the booming voice of God, "Whom shall I send, and who will go for Us?" (v. 8).

With just such pervasiveness the call of God comes to us. It is like a burning firebrand in our hearts that we cannot escape. It was the pervasiveness of God's call that Jeremiah experienced when he said, "There is in my heart as it were a burning fire shut up in my bones, and I am weary with holding it in, and I cannot" (20:9, RSV). It was the pervasiveness of God's call that Paul experienced when he cried out, "For woe is me if I do not preach the gospel" (1 Cor. 9:16, NASB). It was the pervasiveness of God's call that pursued Jonah until in the belly of the great fish he simply had to give in, which sought Elijah in the cave of seclusion and called him back to service.

What does this mean for us? Once you experience the call of God and see those things before you which God has planned, once through the Spirit of God you get a taste of those things which eyes have not seen nor ears heard nor the human mind conceived, then you will never be satisfied with any other way. You will find no peace until you say with Isaiah, "Here am I. Send me!" (v. 8).

3. *Problem*

At this point, a problem surfaced. When God's call became apparent, Isaiah was immediately overwhelmed by a sense of inadequacy. He was to take the message of a holy God to an unholy nation. He was to stand up in the midst of the world's darkness and hold up the light. That was the problem. He didn't think he could handle the job. His inadequacy was expressed in his poignant cry: "Woe is me, for I am ruined! Because I am a man of unclean lips, and I live among a people of unclean lips" (v. 5, NASB).

This cry of inadequacy always erupts from within when God's call comes. We saw it in Moses, in Gideon, in Jeremiah, in Amos, in Elijah. From Moses' day until ours, the problem of responding to God's challenge for our lives has always been that we simply do not feel ourselves to be adequate to the task.

Paul said to the Corinthians, "But we have this treasure in

earthen vessels, that the surpassing greatness of the power may be of God and not from ourselves" (2 Cor. 4:7). With one voice, we cry out, "We *are* earthen vessels. Of what use can we be to God? How can we fulfill the task to which God has called us?"

4. *Provision*

Isaiah learned a lesson that we need to learn today. He learned that when God calls, he will provide all we need to fulfill his call. Two points became very clear to Isaiah as he encountered the challenge of God.

He learned that God is still on his throne. The trauma that Isaiah felt because of the death of King Uzziah is difficult for us to even imagine. Isaiah wondered if the nation would even survive. In the Temple that day Isaiah saw *the* king high and lifted up. Isaiah discovered that although earthly kings may come and go in endless procession, *the* King—Yahweh—would rule forever and ever.

Isaiah also learned that God would touch him at the very point of his need. Isaiah's problem was that he was a man of sinful lips. As soon as Isaiah voiced this need, the seraphim of God took the burning coal and placed it upon his lips. Do you understand what this means? God will provide for us at the very point of our weakness. For our sinfulness there is his holiness. For our weakness there is his strength. For our timidity there is his boldness.

Hudson Taylor, one of history's greatest exemplars of faith, summed it up in one sentence: "God's work in God's way will never lack supplies." When we look at ourselves we say, "I can't." That is the problem. When we look at God we know that he "is able to do exceeding abundantly beyond all that we ask or think, according to the power that works within us" (Eph. 3:20). That is the provision.

When God calls, God provides. That's why every Christian can respond to the call of God with this confident response: "Here am I. Send me!"

JEREMIAH

24. When You're Ready to Quit

Jeremiah 9:2

One cannot read the story of Jeremiah without realizing that life was not a bouquet of roses for this great prophet of God. From his call in 626 BC, to the fall of his beloved Jerusalem in 586 BC, this prophet from Anathoth moved in the tragic circumstances of a lonely life. His task was to call his people to repentance. As he carried out this task he found himself alienated from his friends, antagonized by his enemies, and afflicted by the hostility of his people. Our text describes a time when, awed by the opposition and defeated by discouragement, Jeremiah wanted to quit. He wanted to abandon his God-given task and settle for a life of seclusion. "O," he said, "that I had in the desert a wayfarer's lodging place, that I might leave my people and go away from them!" (RSV). Perhaps no other verse in the book gives us such an open window into the soul of this great prophet.

Isn't this verse also a window into our own soul? Is there anything which decays our stability, destroys our productivity, and defuses our ability like discouragement? How often we find ourselves in Jeremiah's shoes, confronted by the great enemy discouragement. And how often do we like Jeremiah, overcome by such discouragement, long for a wayfarer's lodging place in the desert where we can go away and hide.

Discouragement faces us almost every day as we carry out the Lord's work. Why then should we keep going? Why can't we settle for a wayfarer's lodging place?

1. *Because of the Challenge Within*

We cannot settle for a wayfarer's lodging place because of the inner call of God. Jeremiah was a man with a challenge. From his earliest days, when his father carried out the priestly functions at Anathoth, Jeremiah had been in close communion with God. Out of that experience with God, Jeremiah discovered a challenge which God had planted deep within him. This challenge is explained in Jeremiah 1:4-5, NASB; "Now the word of the Lord came to me saying, 'Before I formed you in the womb I knew you, and before you were born I consecrated you; I have appointed you a prophet to the nations.' " The challenge is further defined in verses 9-10. Jeremiah was a man with a challenge.

Although Jeremiah felt inadequate to the task, although he was unsuccessful at times, although the people remained indifferent and no one seemed to care, Jeremiah could not settle for a wayfarer's resting place because he had the challenge of God burning within his heart, and he could not escape it. In his own words, "But if I say, 'I will not remember Him or speak any more in His name,' Then in my heart it becomes like a burning fire shut up in my bones; and I am weary of holding it in, and I cannot endure it" (Jer. 20:9, NASB).

If there is any phrase which characterizes the Christian life, it is that we are people with a mission. "Go ye into all the world, and preach the gospel to every creature" (Mark. 16:15, KJV) is the inescapable mandate of the Christian life.

A gray-haired Sunday School teacher became ill after many years of faithful teaching. The doctor told him he had cancer. He had only a short time to live. When his pastor visited him, the dear saint said, "Pastor, do you know what I'd like to do more than anything else in the world? I'd like to go back and teach my men's Bible class just one more time. I want to tell them that not only is Jesus Christ a wonderful Savior to live by, but he is also a wonderful Savior to die by."

Our challenge is to proclaim that message to the world. Regardless of how people respond, regardless of their hostility and indifference, regardless of their lack of understanding, we cannot quit and settle for a wayfarer's resting place because that challenge is burning in our hearts, and we cannot escape it.

2. *Because of the Need Without*

We cannot settle for a wayfarer's resting place because of the outer need. How vividly this appeared to Jeremiah is evident in his prophecy. As he looked at those around him, his heart was burdened by their spiritual condition. They had turned from God. They were wasting their lives. They were traveling down a pathway that would ultimately lead to their destruction. Jeremiah could not give up, even when he wanted to, because he was compelled by this need around him to keep going.

The need of the world around us is just as evident in our day. When a teacher asked one of her students to tell the class the shape of the world, the little girl responded, "My daddy says that it is in the worst shape it has ever been in." The little girl was right. Never have there been more broken homes, more ruined lives, more subtle temptations, more atrocious manifestations of sin, and more opportunities for the power of evil than in our generation. Never has a generation of people had a greater need for God than ours.

Before you give up and find a wayfarer's resting place, ask yourself this question, "If we don't do something about this need, who will?"

Jesus described the compelling impetus of this need around us in his story of the shepherd and his sheep (Luke 15). At evening, when the shepherd counted his sheep, ninety-nine were safe in the pen. That's a pretty good percentage. Ninety-nine percent is not bad. However, the shepherd was not concerned about percentages. He was concerned about lost sheep. So he went out immediately and searched diligently until he found the one lost sheep. Then, he laid it on his shoulders and called his friends to rejoice with him for this one lost sheep had been found.

Even if there is only one sheep that is lost, only one person who is in need, only one individual who is hurting, only one Christian who is straying, we still have to keep going. The need without calls us out of our discouragement.

3. *Because We Have the Answer for the Need*

We cannot settle for a wayfarer's resting place because we have the answer for the need of our world. Jesus Christ is the answer. Every spiritual need can be met by this one who is the Bread of life.

The Baton Rouge Gideon Camp sponsored a Gideon Day at Angola Penitentiary. They took Bibles into the cells of the prisoners to tell them about the love of God. One of these Gideons was named Luther. When he walked into Charlie Frazier's cell, the prisoner started cursing him. Charlie Frazier was a notorious criminal, having been in solitary confinement for twelve years. He didn't want to talk to anybody, and he didn't want to talk about God. So he ordered Luther to get out. "You religious people come down and talk about the love of God. It's easy for you. Just get out."

Luther put his hand on Frazier's shoulder, looked him in the eyes, and said, "Fellow, I just want to tell you that I love you." Frazier ordered Luther out of the cell again. He left, but as he did, he laid a Bible on the bunk. "This is the Word of God," he said in parting. "I hope you read it."

A few days later, Luther received a phone call from the chaplain at Angola Penitentiary. He informed Luther that Charlie Frazier had been converted to Jesus Christ. Frazier became superintendent of the Sunday School at Angola Penitentiary, a position he held until stricken with cancer. After Frazier's death, the Louisiana attorney general was quoted as saying in the New Orleans paper, "We don't know what changed Frazier. He was a notorious criminal. He killed two guards in an attempt to escape from our penitentiary, but in the past few years he has been a new man. I don't know what came over him, but whatever it was changed his life."[25]

We know what it was. It was Christ, for he is the answer to man's deepest needs. That's why we must never quit.

LAMENTATIONS

25. Two Mathematical Mistakes

Lamentations 1:9

A man gave this testimony of his life: "I have made two mistakes in life, and both mistakes are mathematical. I misjudged the brevity of life and the length of eternity."

Many centuries before a prophet of Israel gave the same testimony about his contemporaries. "She did not consider her future;" the prophet said, "Therefore she has fallen astonishingly."

Who was this prophet, and what do we know about his sorrowful eulogy over Jerusalem which has come to us in the Book of Lamentations? Tradition affirms—although we cannot be certain—that Jeremiah is the prophet who gave us Lamentations. Many modern scholars have questioned that position, but the strong tradition still persists. What we do know is that the author seems to have been an eyewitness to the destruction of Jerusalem, that these words were uttered shortly after 586 BC, and that the prophet was brokenhearted by the tragic destruction of his beloved city. Lamentations is, as one scholar expressed it, "a cloudburst of grief, a river of tears, a sea of sobs."[26] Reading the book is like attending the funeral of a dear friend. Lamentations is perhaps the most solemn soliloquy in all of the Scriptures.

Two themes emerge from the book: the failure of Judah, and the faithfulness of Yahweh. The latter is pronounced in Lamentations 3:22-23. The former is summarized in our text. Judah made two mistakes, and both were mathematical: she misjudged the brevity of life and the length of eternity. "She did not consider her future."

1. *The Brevity of Life*

The brevity of life is a fact that is illustrated throughout Scripture. The writer of Proverbs said, "Do not boast about tomorrow, for you do not know what a day may bring forth" (Prov. 27:1, NASB). "My days," said Job, "are swifter than a weaver's shuttle" (Job 7:6, NASB).

The brevity of life was illustrated in the parable of Jesus about the rich farmer who filled his barns with the abundance of his goods and then sat back to enjoy life. That night he died, and God said unto him, "You fool! This very night your soul is required of you; and now who will own what you have prepared?" (Luke 12:20, NASB).

The brevity of life was also illustrated in James 4:14: "Yet you do not know what your life will be like tomorrow. You are just a vapor that appears for a little while and then vanishes away." The verbs "appear" and "vanish" were used by Aristotle to refer to the appearance and disappearance of a flock of birds as they swept across the sky. You don't see them. Then you do. Then you see them no more. They are here one moment; gone the next. So is life, James says. Life passes quickly, as an unknown author has written.

When as a child I laughed and wept,
  Time crept.
When as a youth, I dreamed and talked,
  Time walked.
When I became a full-grown man,
  Time ran.
When older still I grew,
  Time flew.
Soon I shall find in traveling on,
  Time gone.

Because of the brevity of life, today is packed full of eternal significance. Today is the time for coming to terms with God. Today is the time for building relationships with our children. Today is the time for expressing our love for our mates. Today is the time for dealing with our bad habits. Today is the time for sharing our witness with a friend. Yesterday is a canceled check. Tomorrow is a promissory note. Only today is legal tender.

2. *The Length of Eternity*

Because of the brevity of life, today is the doorway into eternity. In contrast to today which quickly passes, eternity is forever. As we consider our future, we not only need to live life to the fullest today. We also need to prepare for what follows life on this earth.

Some suggest that there is nothing after life. The bold affirmation of the Bible, supported by the deepest longing of all people of all ages, is that there is indeed life after life. The Bible reminds us that how we live this life will determine what we experience in that life. We can't get into heaven then unless heaven gets into us now!

John Wesley, the founding father of Methodism, was asked one day, "If you knew that the Lord would come tomorrow night, how would you spend the day?" Wesley answered, "I would spend it just as I intended to spend it. I would preach tonight at Gloucester, and again tomorrow morning. After that, I would ride to Tewkesbury, preach in the afternoon, and meet the Society in the evening. I would spend the last hours of the evening with my Christian brother, Martin. I would talk with him about the Lord, pray with his family, retire to my room at ten o'clock, commend myself to my Heavenly Father, and wake up in glory!"

There was a man who was ready. Wesley was so present with God in the present that if God's future were to break into today, not one item on the agenda of his life would have to be changed.

For those who, aware of the brevity of life and the length of eternity, live in the present in a state of preparedness for the future, the testimony of their lives is, "Even so, come, Lord Jesus." Those who ignore these realities will be marked throughout all eternity with this excruciating epitaph of the eulogists of Judah: "She did not consider her future."

EZEKIEL

26. Can These Bones Live?

Ezekiel 37:1-10

Ezekiel is a strange book—a book of weird images and wild flights of imagination. The book was so disturbing to the Jews because of its inconsistencies with the Torah that they would not allow parts of the book to be read in the synagogue. Most of us don't understand the book well enough to be disturbed about it. It is one of the most enigmatic books of the Bible.

The one section of the book about which we are familiar is the picture of the prophet in the valley of the dry bones. The hand of the Lord picked up Ezekiel and set him down in the midst of a vast valley. All around him, everywhere he looked, Ezekiel could see nothing but dry bones. The Lord asked him the piercing question which I want us to answer, "Can these bones live?" (v. 3).

1. *The Question*

That question can be asked about many different "bones" in our churches today.

That question can be asked about the *jawbones* of the church. Jawbones are those who do a lot of talking, but do nothing to back up their talk. They talk the talk, but they don't walk the walk.

Soren Kierkegaard's parable about the geese is a beautiful illustration of these jawbones. Every seventh day these geese would parade to a corner of the yard where their most eloquent orator sat upon the fence and spoke about the wonders of being a goose. He told them the great things their forefathers had done. He described the flight of their illustrious predecessors. He spoke of the mercy of the Creator who had given geese wings and the instinct to fly. The geese were deeply impressed by the eloquent oration. They nodded their heads solemnly, said amen, and even applauded. There was one thing, however, that they never did. They didn't fly. Instead, they returned to their dinners and the security of their barnyards.

How like Christians in our churches today. We testify to our dedication. We just don't demonstrate it in our lives. We talk the talk, but we don't walk the walk. As we look at all the jawbones in today's churches, the question comes to our lips, "Can these bones live?"

This question can be asked, also, about the *wishbones* of the church. Wishbones are those who realize it takes more than talk; they just wish someone else would do it. Our churches are filled with wishbones. The older people are tired and wish the young people would take over. The younger people are afraid they are not competent enough, and they wish the older folks would do the work. We just sit and wish while the work goes undone, and the opportunities slip by, and lives slip away from the doors of heaven. As we look at all the wishbones in the church, the question comes to our lips, "Can these bones live?"

This question can also be asked about the *knucklebones* of the church. These are the complainers. They don't do anything themselves; but they knock anyone else who tries to. They are always ready with their favorite line, "We never did it that way before."

When Freddie Hutchinson was manager of the Cincinnati Reds, he became weary of his team's complaints about the heat at the park. He called a team meeting. He warned that the next guy who complained about the heat would be fined $100. The next day Art Fowler was pitching for the Reds. It was a scorcher of a day. After six innings on the mound, Fowler came into the dugout, sprawled out, closed his eyes, poured a cup of water on his head, and moaned, "Man, it is really hot." He opened his eyes to find himself face to face with a steaming Freddie Hutchinson. Without missing a beat,

Fowler added, "And that's just the way I like it!"

People who gripe in the church do so because things are not the way they like them. As we see these knucklebones in today's churches, the question again comes to our lips, "Can these bones live?"

This question can also be asked about the *dry bones* in the church. When Ezekiel was carried to the valley, he said that he was surrounded by dry bones. These were not just dead people, but people who had been dead so long that the bones had become dry, scorched, and bleached by the sun. These were bones which no longer had any life in them.

In the churches today, there are many dry bones who are dead spiritually. Some have been dead so long that they have become completely dried out by the scorching sun of indifference. As we witness the valley of dry bones, knucklebones, wishbones, and jawbones in today's churches, the question comes to our lips, "Can these bones live?

2. *The Answer*

Thank God we have an answer to give! The good news of God's Word is that dry bones can live again. Even when people and causes and forces are like the dry bones Ezekiel witnessed in the valley, when God's Spirit begins to do his work, things come alive.

This is the message that was prefigured in the experience in Ezekiel's valley. The array of dry bones around him seemed to present a helpless and hopeless situation. But then God's Spirit went to work. The foot bones connected to the ankle bones, and to the leg bones, and to the hip bones, and to the back and arms and neck and head. Then sinews and flesh came upon them. Then the wind came and filled them. And they lived! Dry bones, dead, and bleached by the scorching sun, came alive and stood upon their feet as an exceedingly great army. Ezekiel had his answer to the appeal of God. Yes, these bones can live, through the power of God's Spirit.

This message, which was prefigured in Ezekiel's vision and found expression in numerous experiences throughout history, was indelibly printed on the pages of history in concrete, conclusive, once-for-all terms in the resurrection of Jesus Christ. This is the message of the empty tomb, the pulsebeat of Christianity, the hope of the world.

That dark day after Calvary, Jesus' body was laid in the tomb, for he was dead. Say it over and over again until the message sinks into your mind and sends the chill of despair racing up and down your spine. Jesus was dead! All the hopes of all the centuries which the disciples had lodged in the life of their Messiah seemed to have died with him. But then God went to work. Before God's Spirit was through, Jesus was again walking with the disciples as their companion, ascending before them as their Lord, promising to come again as their King. That is the message of the empty tomb. God can bring life out of that which appears to be dead.

This message prefigured in Ezekiel's valley and proclaimed in Christ's resurrection is a message for you. When God's Spirit goes to work in your life, things can come alive. Broken homes can be repaired. Broken lives can be restored. Broken dreams can be rekindled.

God is ready to help you put the pieces back together in your life and renew your spirit. He is ready to gather all the jawbones, wishbones, knucklebones, and dry bones in your church and make them come alive. He is ready to shine the beam of his resurrection power into the grave of your broken dreams and help you live again. When God's Spirit goes to work, things come alive!

DANIEL

27. Getting Out of the Passive Voice

Daniel 6:10

A rather illiterate salesman for a company wrote a letter to his boss which said, "Dere Boss: I dun seen this outfit which they ain't never bot a dim's wuth of nuthin from us, and I sole them a couple hunert thousand dollars wuth of guds. Now I'm gwine to Chawgo."

Two days later a second letter arrived at the home office from the same salesman which said: "Dere Boss: I cum hear and sole them half a milyon."

Both letters were posted on the bulletin board with a note appended by the company president which said: "Dere Selsmen: We been spendin' to much time hear trying to spel instead of trying to sel. Let's watch these letters from Gooch who is on the rode doing a grate job for us and you go out and do like he dun!"

When you are a salesman for a firm, selling is not something simply to talk about. It is something you need to do, for your actions will speak louder than your words.

This truth also applies to our spiritual lives. The most evident problem with Christians today is not that we do evil, but that we do nothing at all. We're like the lady on whose tombstone was written the words:

Here lie the bones of Nancy Jones.
For her, life held no terrors.
She lived an old maid.
She died an old maid.
No hits, no runs, no errors!

The greatest challenge facing us today is to get out of the

passive voice into the active voice, to become doers of the word rather than hearers only.

What a dynamic example of this kind of active living was young Daniel. Daniel had enemies at court who were determined to disgrace him. They persuaded King Darius to sign a decree forbiding worship to anyone but him for thirty days. As soon as the document was signed, Daniel's enemies watched him to see what he would do. What did he do? He acted.

1. *Calmly*

Daniel acted calmly. When he knew that the document had been signed, Daniel entered his house to pray and give thanks before God. Quickly, without hesitation, and quietly, without fanfare, Daniel shifted into the active voice.

Action does not have to be dramatic or extreme in order to be effective. Sometimes the calm, quiet movement of an unassuming child of God makes the most profound impact.

When Dick Sheppard began his ministry in East London, he thought very highly of his ministerial skills. He felt that in just a short while he could do a lot for the working classes. Sheppard began seeing an old man whose days often ended in drunkenness and whose wife was suffering from her burden. Sheppard fed the old gentleman his best theology. The only result, reported Sheppard, was that "we bored the old gentleman stiff."

Some months later, Sheppard heard that the man had dramatically changed. He had overcome his drunkenness and was once again living a life of usefulness. During those months the old man had been visited by an elderly clergyman named Strickland who was a noticeably unattractive man and whom Sheppard felt had no spiritual gifts at all.

Curiosity led Sheppard to call on the man to see what had happened. All the old man talked about was Reverend Strickland's visits. Sheppard responded, "Mr. Strickland doesn't have much to say for himself, does he?" "No," was the reply, "he doesn't have much to say, and sometimes I don't know what to say to him, but when he is gone I kind of say to myself that it seems as if Jesus of Nazareth had passed by."[27]

Sometimes the calm action demonstrated by Daniel leaves the distinct impression that it is as if Jesus of Nazareth had passed by.

2. *Courageously*

Daniel also acted courageously. Daniel was aware of the decree signed by the king. He was also aware of the consequences of his action. Nevertheless, Daniel prayed and gave thanks before God.

Harry Emerson Fosdick once said, "There are two kinds of faith in God. One says if—if all goes well, if life is hopeful, prosperous and happy, then I will believe in God; the other says though—though the forces of evil triumph, though everything goes wrong, and Gethsemane comes and the cross looms, nevertheless, I will believe in God."[28]

Anyone can act for God when everything is going your way. But when opposition arises and suffering looms before us, only the brave in spirit act.

3. *Consistently*

Further, Daniel acted consistently. The Bible tells us that when the document was signed, he prayed and gave thanks to God, "as he had been doing previously."

An oft quoted statement is usually attributed to Calvin Coolidge: "Press on: Nothing in the world takes the place of persistence. Talent will not; nothing is more common than unsuccessful men with talent. Genius will not; unrewarded genius is almost a proverb. Education will not; the world is full of educated derelicts. Persistence and determination alone are omnipotent."

The key in getting out of the passive voice is consistency. Outward circumstances must be outvoted by inner commitment. Danger must be defeated by discipline.

4. *Conclusion*

Hoping to inspire his workers to action, a San Francisco executive posted a number of signs reading "Do it Now" throughout his factory and offices. When he was asked several weeks later how his staff reacted, he shook his head sadly. "I don't even like to talk about it," he said. "The cashier skipped with $5,000. The head accountant eloped with the best secretary I ever had. Three typists asked for a raise. The factory workers voted to go on strike. And the office boy joined the Navy!"

It is not that kind of action I want to spur you to, but calm, courageous, consistent action for God when I say that we need to follow Daniel's example and get out of the passive voice.

HOSEA

28. When God's People Sin

Hosea 5:1-15

Calvin Coolidge was known as a man of few words, a fact confirmed in a conversation he had with his wife one day. Coolidge returned from a church service which his wife had not attended. She asked, "Calvin, what did the preacher talk about today?" "Sin," he replied. "What did the pastor say about sin?" she asked further. Coolidge answered, "He was against it!"

In our best moments, all of us would concur with that evaluation of sin. Nevertheless, we often allow sin to set up residence in our lives. It may be the obvious sins of rebellion that led one father to say to his boy, "Son, this is the third fatted calf I've killed for you this week. When are you going to settle down?" Or it could be the gray sins of indifference, inertia, and omission. Of whatever variety, sin is a reality even in the life of God's children.

It was sin in the life of God's children in Israel that evoked the prophetic message we know as Hosea. Hosea was born in the Northern Kingdom, Israel, and spent his life there. It was there he prophesied. He was the son of Beeri (1:1), married to Gomer, and the father of three children. The period in which he prophesied is described in 2 Kings 14:23 to 18:12. It was a time of chaotic disorder internally and a time of a dramatic shift of power internationally.

The first of the book focuses on a personal problem in Hosea's life which became the backdrop for his prophecy to the nation. Hosea's experience with his wife Gomer, who turned from him to an adulterous relationship with other men, led Hosea to a disturbing discovery. Israel had done the same thing to God that Gomer had done to him. Hosea thereby became the instrument by which God called Israel back to the faith.

What was the problem? God's people had sinned. Hosea's message about sin is one we need to hear today.

1. *The Result of Sin*

A minister announced to his congregation that there were 375 specific sins. One of his parishioners wanted a list after the service, to make sure he wasn't missing anything! Actually, there is nothing frivolous about sin. It will eventually destroy everything beautiful and worthwhile in your life.

What does sin do? What are the results of sin in the lives of God's children?

Sin *distorts our lives*. Paul says in Romans 6:23 that the wages of sin is death. That means everytime we sin, something dies. The personal effect of sin is that our lives are robbed of their joy and fulfillment.

This note of personal destruction is sounded throughout our text. "Israel and Ephraim stumble in their iniquity" (v. 5). "Now the new moon will devour them with their land" (v. 7). "Ephraim will become a desolation in the day of rebuke" (v. 9). Sin deprives us of the joy of our salvation.

Sin also *disrupts our relationship with God*. This note of spiritual separation is sounded throughout Hosea's prophecy. "Their deeds will not allow them to return to their God" (v. 4). "They do not know the Lord" (v. 4). "They will go with their flocks and herds to seek the Lord, but they will not find Him" (v. 6). "I will go away and return to My place" (v. 15). Separation from God's presence, separation from God's power, separation from God's purpose, separation from God's provision—that is the ultimate tragic result of our sin.

Wayne Dehoney tells of two portraits that Rembrandt painted of himself. The first, as a young man, shows him as a handsome youth with the lamp of love burning in his eyes. He is a man full of potential whose creative genius is evident. Twenty years later, he painted another portrait of himself.

During these twenty years Rembrandt had denied himself no pleasure. As a libertine, he sought out every delight. The second self-portrait shows the mark of sin on his life for the joy and potential of the young man has been replaced by a face marked with the lines of debaucherous living, with eyes dull and without vision.[29]

That is what sin does to us. As James put it in his epistle, "Then when lust has conceived, it gives birth to sin; and when sin is accomplished, it brings forth death" (Jas. 1:15, NASB).

2. *The Remedy for Sin*

If Hosea ceased his prophetic message of judgment with verse 14, the pain of it would be more than we could bear. Thank God for the word *until*. God said, "I will go away and return to My place until . . ." (v. 15). *Until* is a word of hope. It is a word of promise. It is a word that opens the door to a second chance. Sin will destroy our lives and disrupt our relationship with God *until*. Until what? What is the remedy for sin? Hosea suggests two steps.

The first step is to *repent*: "Until they acknowledge their guilt" (v. 15). That is the step that leads to reconciliation with God. As I visited in a home recently, the wife was describing the chaotic condition that prevailed there. Finally, she said, "Pastor, all I can say is that things are not as they should be." To come to the point where you know things are not as they should be, and you want to do something about it—that is the first step that leads to reconciliation.

The second step is *return*: "Until they . . . seek My face" (v. 15). Reconciliation with God comes not only when we turn from our sin but also when we turn to him.

The story of the prodigal son in Luke 15 beautifully illustrates the twofold movement that leads to restoration. The Gospel writer tells us, "But when he came to his senses, he said, 'How many of my father's hired men have more than enough bread, but I am dying here with hunger!' " (Luke 15:17, NASB). That is repentance. Then notice the next step: "I will get up and go to my father" (v. 18). That is returning to

God. Reconciliation comes not only when we realize that it is wrong to be in the far country. Reconciliation comes when we realize that it is right to be with the Father.

The Book of Hosea which one man calls "a book for backsliders" is a book for our day. This prophetic message needs to be sounded to our people. The end of sin is destruction and separation from God. Life is found when we turn from our sin, and turn back to him.

JOEL

29. Passing the Torch

Joel 1:3

Recently I read of an interesting contrast made between two men in Northampton, Massachusetts, in the early 1700s. One was a preacher named Jonathan Edwards. The other was an unbeliever named Max Jukes.

Jonathan Edwards married a devout Christian girl and from their union came 729 descendants. Of these, 300 were ministers, 65 were college professors, 13 were university presidents, 60 were authors of good books, 3 were United States congressmen, and one was vice-president of the United States. Most made a significant contribution to society.

Max Jukes, who lived close to Jonathan Edwards, was an unbeliever. He married an unbeliever and from their union came 1,026 descendants. Of these, 300 died early in life, 100 went to prison for an average of 13 years apiece, 200 were prostitutes, and 100 were alcoholics. The descendants of this man cost the state more than a million dollars to care for them.

I have no way of checking the accuracy of these figures. Nevertheless, these facts should raise in our minds some interesting questions: *How will our children turn out? And what is the primary force which molds the life of an individual and determines what he will accomplish in life?* I believe that the answer to those questions is a child's parents.

A cartoon showed a kangaroo with a baby kangaroo peeping out of the pouch. This caption was at the bottom: "His mother determines his point of view." It's true. Like no other factor in a child's life, the parents will determine his point of view in life. Like father, like son. Like mother, like daughter. That is a truth written large in human history.

This is the point that Joel makes in the opening words of his prophecy. The devastation of locusts to which Joel refers was more than a physical phenomenon. It was a spiritual revelation to the Hebrew people. The locust plague was a revelation of the power of God's judgment, and a reminder of the necessity of faith. It provided God's people a spiritual lesson which must never be forgotten. Joel, therefore, challenged his contemporaries to pass on this message from generation to generation.

One of the most dramatic sports events is the lighting of the torch at the olympic games which symbolizes the passing on of a great tradition. Even more important is the passing of the torch of faith from one generation to the next. The responsibility to do this rests squarely upon the shoulders of parents. How can we pass the torch of faith to our children?

1. *Declare It*

First, we must declare our faith to our children. The home is a classroom in which daily lessons are administered. An important item on the curriculum must be the matter of our faith in God.

Lyle Schaller, in his book *Understanding Tomorrow*, identifies one of the characteristics of our age to be excessive expectations of institutions. To a substantial degree, we parents have turned over to two institutions, the school and the church, the responsibility to develop our children into dedicated, dependable adults. Tests reveal that these expectations placed on our institutions far exceed their capabilities.[30] Institutions which were meant to supplement what we do in the home have been expected to replace what we do in the home. However, we simply cannot delegate to other institutions the responsibilities that God intended to be assumed by the home.

If your children are to learn to love God, you have to teach them in the home. If they are to become men and women of faith, you have to develop them in the home. If they are to love and understand the Word of God, you have to teach it in the home.

James Dobson tells of a study on the early childhoods of

inmates at a state prison in Arizona. The researchers were hoping to discover a common characteristic which the prisoners shared in hopes this would give some insight into the cause of antisocial behavior. Initially, the researchers assumed poverty would be the common thread. Such was not the case, for the prisoners came from many different socioeconomic levels. The one fundamental characteristic shared by the men was an absence of adult contact in their early home lives. As children, they spent most of their time in the company of peers, or alone. The conclusion of the study was that there is no substitute for loving, parental leadership in the early development of children.[31]

To pass on the torch of faith to our children we must declare to them the truth of our faith.

2. *Demonstrate It*

Our responsibility goes deeper. Not only must we declare our faith; we must also demonstrate it.

Josh Billings, the American humorist, once said, "Train up a child in the way he should go; and walk there yourself once in a while!" That's good advice. The single most powerful impact that you have on your children is not what you say, but what you do; not the convictions you claim but the convictions you really have as evidenced by the way you live your life.

Several years ago, after preaching a sermon on fathers, I received a letter from Deanna Longshore, a young person in my church, who told me of the influence of her father on her life. She concluded her letter with this paragraph: "I have a good solid concept of God as my Heavenly Father. And the reason I do is because of my earthly father. It's because of Daddy that I am able to love God and relate to him as my Father."

You can't do anything about your ancestors. But you can do something about your descendants. By declaring your faith to your children, and by demonstrating your faith before your children, you can pass the torch to them.

AMOS

30. The Responsibility of Privilege

Amos 3:2

A businessman was interviewing a young man as a prospective employee. He told the young man, "What I need is someone who is responsible." "I'm your man, then," the young man responded, "At the place I worked before, whenever something went wrong, they always said I was responsible."

Responsibility is not a word we hear much about anymore. Our favorite words are privilege and opportunity and freedom and rights. We don't like to talk about responsibility and obligation and duties.

We have a way of trying to slip out of responsibility for what we are. Will Rogers once said, "The history of America can be written in three phases: the passing of the Indian, the passing of the Buffalo, and the passing of the buck!" A young man who came home with a black eye and bloody nose explained to his mother, "The fight started when Bob hit me back." When Moses came down from the mountain where he had received the Commandments from God, he found the Hebrews worshiping a golden calf that Aaron had made for them. When Moses demanded an explanation, Aaron said, "I took the gold that the people gave me (author's translation), and I threw it in the fire, and out came this calf" (Ex. 32:24, NASB). The thread that weaves its way through all three of these experiences is the same: we have a tendency to blame others for what we are.

The message of God's Word, however, is that we and we alone are ultimately responsible for what we are. We are not responsible for everything that happens to us, but we are responsible for how we respond to what happens to us. We and we alone are responsible for whether we use the circumstances of our life as building blocks to success or allow them to become stumbling stones that lead to failure.

Responsibility is a key note of Amos' message. The word *Amos* means burden bearer. It is a fitting name for this prophet of the eighth century BC, for he bore the burden on his heart for the poor and mistreated of Israel. Israel was prospering in every way. The result was a spirit of self-sufficiency and smug complacency. Amos shattered the complacency of the people with a reminder of their responsibility to God and to their countrymen whom they were defrauding. The judgment of God would come, Amos declared, because they had lost sight of their responsibility.

In our text, which may be the most important passage in the book, Amos took the idea of responsibility a step further. What he said was, "The greater the privilege, the greater responsibility." The New Testament parallel to this declaration is found in James 3:1: "Dear brothers, don't be too eager to tell others their faults, for we all make many mistakes; and when we teachers of religion who should know better, do wrong, our punishment will be greater than it would be for others" (author's translation).

In our day in which we thrive on the privileges which are ours, we need to be reminded of the responsibility of privilege.

1. *Our Relationship with God*

The greater the privilege, the greater the responsibility. This truth applies, first, to our relationship to God.

If any people were ever privileged in their relationship with God, it was the Hebrew people. It was the Hebrew people whom God chose as his instruments of grace. It was the Hebrew people whom he delivered from Egyptian slavery. It was the Hebrew people with whom he had made a covenant and to whom he had given his written law. It was the Hebrews whom God had ushered into their Promised Land. What a privileged people the Hebrews were! To the Hebrews God said through his prophet Amos, "You only have I chosen among all the families of the earth" (3:2, NASB). But along with the privilege came the responsibility to live righteously before God.

Study again the narrative of the covenant relationship God made with Israel at Sinai, and you will discover that it was a reciprocal agreement. God promised certain things to the Hebrews, and he demanded certain things of them. The Ten Commandments were the stipulations by which the covenant relationship with Israel was to be regulated. In order to exist in a relationship with a holy God, they, too, had to be holy.

The Hebrew people had the privilege of knowing how God wanted them to live. Instead, "they rejected the law of the Lord and have not kept His statues" (Amos 2:4, NASB). That's why Amos said in our text, "You only have I chosen among all the families of the earth; therefore, I will punish you for all your iniquities." Because we know what God demands, we should live in righteousness. That's the responsibility of privilege.

2. *Our Relationship with Others*

The greater the privilege, the greater the responsibility. This truth applies also to our relationship with others.

The people in Amos' day were prospering in every way. They were blessed with incomparable material blessings. The hand of the Lord was upon them. What a privileged people the Hebrews were! To the Hebrews God said through his prophet Amos, "You only have I chosen among all the families of the earth" (3:2, NASB). But along with the privilege came the responsibility to be instruments of grace to others.

Look again at the Ten Commandments, the stipulations by which the covenant relationship with God was to be regulated, and you will see that there was not only a vertical dimension but also a horizontal dimension. Because of the covenant God made with them, the Hebrew people not only had a responsibility to live in righteousness before him. They also had the responsibility to live in love toward their neighbor.

The Hebrew people had the privilege of knowing how God wanted them to relate to their neighbors. Instead, "they sell the righteous for money and the needy for a pair of sandals" (Amos 2:6, NASB). That's why Amos said in our text, "You only have I chosen among all the families of the earth; therefore, I will punish you for all your iniquities." Because we know what God demands, we should live in love. That's the responsibility of privilege.

3. *Conclusion*

Two boys were talking about doctors and operations. One asked, "Why do doctors wear masks when they do surgery?" After thinking about it for a moment, the other boy answered, "That way, if they mess up, the patient won't know who did it!"

There is no mask you can hide behind if you mess up your life. It is your life, and you are responsible for what you do with it. In our relationship with God, we are to live in righteousness. In our relationship with others, we are to live in love. That is the responsibility of privilege.

OBADIAH

31. The Echo Principle

Obadiah 15b

One of the most remarkable mysteries of nature is the bat. These strange creatures fly miles underground, swooping through dark caverns, yet they never strike the walls. Until recently, we did not know how they did it. Scientists captured a group of bats to conduct some experiments with them. The scientists stretched wire across a long room and sent the bats through it. They never struck a wire. The scientists blindfolded the bats, thinking that maybe they were able to see in the dark. When the blindfolded bats were sent through the room, they again flew with perfect precision, never touching the sides of the room or the wires stretched across them. When the mouths and ears of the bats were taped shut, different results were seen. With their eyes wide open, the bats crashed into both wires and wall. Further investigation revealed that the bats sounded a high, shrill note when they started to fly. The sound created vibrations which echoed back from any object in their path. The highly sensitive ears of the bat were receivers for the echoed sound. What they sent out came back to them. The echo principle became the tool for the flight of the bats.

The Bible repeatedly declares that the echo principle is a basic principle of life. The writer of Ecclesiastes said, "Cast your bread on the surface of the waters, for you will find it after many days" (Eccl. 11:1, NASB). Jesus told his disciples, "By your standard of measure it shall be measured to you" (Mark 4:24). Paul declared to the Galatians, "Do not be deceived, God is not mocked; for whatever a man sows, this he will also reap" (Gal. 6:7).

The echo principle is passionately proclaimed by one of the most unusual of the Old Testament prophets, Obadiah.

Who was Obadiah? The name *Obadiah* means worshiper or servant of Yahweh. It is a common name in the Old Testament, appearing some twenty times. The prophet Obadiah cannot be identified specifically with any of the other ten or eleven characters by that name in Scripture. We know only that he belonged to Judah, the Southern Kingdom centered in Jerusalem.

The prophecy of Obadiah is a part of the anti-Edom literature which appears throughout the Old Testament (e.g., Gen. 27:39-40; Ps. 137:7; Ezek. 25:12-17; Amos 1:11-12). Some specific atrocity by the Edomites rekindled this anti-Edom spirit and evoked the prophecy of Obadiah in our Old Testament.

A central theme in Obadiah's prophecy is what one man calls "poetic justice." I call it the echo principle. Actions have certain consequences. What you do and say will echo back to you. "As you have done, it will be done to you. Your dealings will return on your own head" (Obad. 15). That is a basic principle of life.

1. *Our Relationship with God*

The echo principle applies to our relationship with God.

When an itinerant preacher was asked to fill the pulpit in a little country church, he took his son along for company. As they entered the church, they noticed an offering box right by the door. The father and son each put a quarter into the offering. That day, only one worshiper showed up, an old gentleman who evidently had little of this world's material wealth. After the sermon, the old gentleman went out to the foyer, emptied the offering box of its contents and gave it to the visiting preacher. Fifty cents in all! When the preacher's son saw what happened, he said to his dad, "If we would have put more into it, we would have gotten more out of it!"

As we give ourselves to God in service, as we learn more about God in study, as we share with God in stewardship, then we will open ourselves to his blessings in our lives. "As you have done, it will be done to you. Your dealings will return on your own head."

2. *Our Relationship with Others*

The echo principle also applies to our relationship with others. This was the heart of Obadiah's message. Edom's hateful treatment of Judah would echo back to her.

A woman who moved to a small town was disturbed by the poor service at the local drug store. She complained to her neighbor, hoping that she would repeat her complaint to the owner. The next time she went to the drug store, the druggist greeted her with a big smile. He told her how glad he was to see her. And he said that he wanted her to know that he would do anything he could to help her and her husband get settled. He then filled her order promptly and efficiently. Later, the woman reported the miraculous change to her friend. She said, "I suppose you passed on my complaint to him about how poor I thought the service was?" "No," responded her neighbor, "in fact, I told him you were amazed at the way he had built up this small town drug store and that you thought it was one of the best run drug stores you'd ever seen!"[32]

Smile, and the world will smile with you. Grump, and it will grump back. "As you have done, it will be done to you. Your dealings will return on your own head."

3. *Our Relationship with Life*

The echo principle is also true of our relationship to life in general. I heard John Claypool say that life is not a gamble but an investment with a predictable relationship between cause and consequence. If life treats you unfairly, it may be in retaliation!

A very wealthy man contracted for a house to be built. Because his business kept him gone most of the time, he told the contractor how much he would pay and then left the details up to him. Seeing an opportunity to make some extra money, the contractor cut every corner that he could. He used cheap material when he could get by with it. His only interest was to make all the money that he could. Finally, the house was completed, and he called the wealthy man to come and check the finished product. It was then that the contractor made a startling discovery. The wealthy benefactor revealed to the contractor that years before the contractor had done a kind deed for him which had enabled him to enter a pathway that led to financial success. "In order to pay you back for your kindness to me," the benefactor said, "I decided to build you a house. I asked you to build it because I knew that you would build a kind of house that you would like to live in. The house is yours!"

So is life for each of us. Each day we are building our lives. We can cut corners and build with cheap material. Or we can build with only the finest, most permanent kind of material. In the end, we must live in the house we have built. "As you have done, it will be done to you. Your dealings will return on your own head."

JONAH

32. Empty Excuses

Jonah 1:10

Elton Trueblood, in probably his most influential book, *The Company of the Committed*, gives this penetrating portrait of the Christian church: "The company of Jesus is not people streaming to a shrine; and it is not people making up an audience for a speaker; it is laborers engaged in the harvesting task of reaching their perplexed and seeking brethren with something so vital that, if it is received, it will change their lives."[33]

Trueblood took that picture right out of the Bible. From the beginning, God said "Come unto me" only so that he could prepare his people to respond to his second command: "Go into the world." God chose his people not only for salvation but also for service. God's people were to be people on mission, and that mission was to proclaim the message of his redeeming love to the world.

God's challenge to go and man's response to it forms the plot for one of the most interesting stories in the Bible, the story of Jonah. No book in the Bible has been so misrepresented, maligned, and misunderstood as the little Book of Jonah. This is more than a fish story! It is a story of God's love for the world, his plan to reach the world, and man's hesitance to be a part of the plan.

Chapter 1 sets the stage for the rest of the book. God said, "Go!" Jonah said, "No!" God told Jonah to proclaim his message. Instead, Jonah was silent. That is a picture repeatedly painted in today's church. God tells us to go, and we say no. God tells us to proclaim his message to a lost world. Instead, we are silent.

Why do we not go as God tells us to do? Why are we silent when we ought to be speaking up for him? That is the question the sailors asked Jonah in our text. When they found out that Jonah was running away from the job his God wanted him to do, they asked, "How could you do this?" Jonah's excuses are the same excuses we use today.

Why do we not go out as witnesses?

1. *Misunderstand the Challenge*

Somewhere in the first few centuries there was a radical change in the understanding of Christian responsibility. Rather than one group of disciples, all facing the same responsibility, the idea of two groups developed. The clergy were those who led worship, who preached and witnessed. The laity were those who attended, received, and watched.

There were differences in gifts in the New Testament, and differences in functions within the church. But the command of Jesus to go out as witnesses is a challenge that comes to every Christian. The witness of the church is not a solo but a chorus.

2. *Misjudge the Urgency*

A life insurance salesman was talking to a customer about a policy. When he finished his presentation, he said, "I believe this is important, but I don't want to force it on you. Go home and sleep on it tonight. And if you wake up in the morning, give me a call!"

There was more truth than humor to that approach. Some people will not wake up in the morning. Every fifteen seconds, someone dies in our country. And the Bible says that if a person dies without Christ, they face the reality of an eternity of separation from God.

3. *Lack the Training*

John Havlik, with the Southern Baptist Home Mission Board, declared that two factors were discovered in launching lay evangelism schools. One was that the average layperson has a greater desire to be used in evangelism than church leaders realize. The other was that laypersons require a great deal more help and equipping than most church leaders believe.[34]

Churches which are reaching people for Christ have at the heart of their program some kind of witness training program. Many techniques are available, but the pastor must take the lead. Paul told the Ephesian Christians that God called pastors and teachers "for the equipping of the saints for the work of service, to the building up of the body of Christ" (Eph. 4:12).

4. *Fear of the Response*

Two men were hunting in the jungles of Africa. Fear and trembling overtook both of them as they saw their first set of lion tracks. One said to the other, "Let's split up. You find out where he went; and I'll find out where he came from!" Not aware he had been conned, the dumber of the hunters began following the tracks. Stumbling through the thick underbrush he came face-to-face with the lion. He passed out. When he woke up, the lion was still there, on his knees praying. With great joy, the hunter leaped up and said, "Thank you, Mr. Lion, for praying for me instead of eating me." "Shut up," replied the lion, "I'm saying grace!"

Now that man had a right to be afraid. But why are we afraid when we go out to witness? Three facts need to be remembered. First, we are not responsible for results. We cannot convict or convince anyone. That is the work of the Holy Spirit. We are responsible simply to share our witness. We can leave the results to God. Second, the Bible tells us that when we go out in his name, God will give us the words to say. Third, the Bible indicates that God is already at work in the lives of those to whom he sends us. You will never talk to anyone that God has not already been dealing with.

If witnessing were an effort totally dependent upon our power, then fear would be understandable. But when we go out, we go out in the power of God!

5. *Absence of Testimony*

When the first telegraph wires were stretched across New England to speed news from New York to Boston, Henry

Thoreau was not impressed. As his friend expounded on the rapidity and clarity with which a message could be transmitted, Thoreau raised a crucial question, "What if we have nothing to say?"

This is what prevents many from witnessing today. They have nothing to say. Either they have never met the Lord, or else their relationship with the Lord is so cold that there is no fire of enthusiasm and excitement in their souls.

A lost world looks at the church today, God's people who have been called to be proclaimers of the Word. As we stand silent before God, the world asks, "How could you do it?" Because we misunderstand the challenge, because we misjudge the urgency of the task, because we are not prepared, because we are afraid, because we have nothing to say—those are the empty excuses that have made the church the real silent majority in today's world.

MICAH

33. *When the Lights Go Out*

Micah 7:7-9

Bruce Laingen, the ranking American hostage held for over a year in Tehran, returned to his home church shortly after the hostages were released. He shared both the faith and doubts which had been a part of his religious pilgrimage during those dark days. At times, he said, all the hostages felt "God must be sitting this one out." On the other hand, he explained that there was no hostage he knew of who failed to draw on religious strength during the long ordeal. What enabled him to make it through, Laingen testified, was his "quiet nightly dialogues with my God."

What do you do when the lights go out? That was a question confronting Micah, the last of the four great prophets of the eighth century. The opening words of Micah put him in the days of Jotham, Ahaz, and Hezekiah which would be about 737-686 BC. Disturbed by the internal situation of low morals, government decadence, and religious indifference, Micah predicted the utter destruction of Jerusalem.

There is little organization to Micah's prophecy, and at times the meaning is difficult to grasp. The mood is very evident, however. It was a dark day in the life of Israel. The judgment of God would come upon the nation, and the lights were going out. While delivering this discouraging message, Micah gave an example of expectant faith. He showed us what faith does when the lights go out.

1. *Accepts*

When the lights go out, faith accepts suffering as an inevitable part of life. Micah said in verse 9, "I will bear the indignation of the Lord."

The old saying, "God had one Son without sin; he didn't have any without suffering" is a stark reminder of the reality of suffering in every life. Our faith is revealed by how we react to suffering.

One lady whose face was marked by many painful experiences in her days, said, "My cheeks have been slapped so much they are quite rosy!" Another man, in response to the statement, "Suffering certainly does color life," declared, "Yes, it does. And I can choose the color!" E. Stanley Jones tells of a basic principle which guided him all through his life. He said, "I determined that I wouldn't bear opposition and difficulties —I would use them."

That's real faith: the perception that each of us at some time walk in the company of the "fraternity of the brokenhearted." Our suffering does not indicate any deficiency in God or any depravity in us. It is simply a part of life on this earth.

2. *Adheres*

When the lights go out, faith adheres. Micah said in verse 7*b*: "I will wait for the God of my salvation." Real faith is patient.

Acts 27 tells the dramatic tale of Paul's adventure at sea. It is a story of storms and shipwreck. In the midst of the experience, the boat was being blown by the wind. Being dark, the sailors could not see. So the Bible says, "And fearing that we might run on the rocks, they let out four anchors from the stern, and prayed for the day to come" (Acts 27:29, RSV). That's faith, the patience to put down the anchors and wait for daybreak to come.

A Christian woman learned one day that her only son had been in a terrible accident and had been rushed to the hospital. When she and her husband arrived at the hospital, he fell by her side with a coronary. When the pastor reached the hospital, this dear saint had her only son in one intensive unit and her husband in another. The pastor was not sure what to say to her, what she would be thinking. As he sat down beside her, the woman said, "Pastor, I'm not going to reach any conclusions about this until God gets through with it."

Faith not only accepts the reality of suffering. Faith also adheres in the midst of suffering by waiting for God to get through with it.

3. *Anticipates*

When the lights go out, faith anticipates. There was a note of optimism in Micah's testimony, a bright glimmer of hope in his proclamation. "Do not rejoice over me, O my enemy," the prophet declared. "Though I fall I will rise; though I dwell in darkness, the Lord is a light for me" (v. 8, NASB). Not just passive acceptance but also active anticipation was the response of the prophet's faith for he said, "I will watch expectantly for the Lord" (v. 7).

This is no shallow optimism which refuses to recognize the reality of suffering. Nor is it a pie-in-the-sky escapism which naively ignores the darkness of the hour. Instead, it is a hope born out of anguish, an optimism colored by reality, a light glimmering ever so faintly in the midst of life's darkness. You catch something of this realistic optimism in a poem by a friend of mine, Patty Neeley. The poem is entitled "To Find the Door."

> As my face hit the wall of obstruction,
> I reverberated back from my problem.
> Glaring at the solid fixture before me,
> The light of my new hope faded.
> But my ears, atuned to a higher calling,
> Heard the voice of Faith.
> It bade me grope along the endless wall
> Till my heart was satisfied with God's solution.
>
> My hand searched every board
> Attempting to discover a final plank.
> Faith once again called, "There exists an exit."
> I, however, could not sense it.

My fingers weary, myself, exhausted,
I leaned upon the next board
Only to feel it give way behind me.
Tumbling through the opening,
My despair was replaced with joy!
Glancing upward, I noticed a doorknob inside.

Wondering how I had passed through a
Door I had not opened.

I turned to catch the voice of Faith
As it echoed through the dark room,
"Only I can open the door from the inside.
Your struggling efforts are in vain
Until you listen to My voice guiding you
To the place I have prepared for you.
When you gave up your desire for life,
The everlasting barrier gave way.
And you have entered My joy!
Continue forth and conquer!"

Squinting into the blankness,
I could not see Him.
Though my eyes perceived nothing,
My heart knew His touch—
His love and His hope.
My belief in Him may at moments falter,
But I know that He yet lives;
His indwelling presence leads me continually.
And one day I shall meet Him whom I have sought
Person to person.

As it was for Bruce Laingen in Tehran, so it was for Micah in Israel—his quiet nightly dialogues with God were what saw him through. God did not remove the reality of suffering. Nor did he remove its hurt. However, he provided hope that the darkness of this temporary failure would eventually be eclipsed by the light of his eternal victory.

NAHUM

34. The Awesomeness of God

Nahum 1:7-8

Tonto and the Lone Ranger were riding across a grassy plateau when they saw a cloud of dust rising up before them. Ten thousand Indians were approaching them from the North. So they turned and headed South. Another cloud of dust rose up before them. Ten thousand Indians were approaching them from the South. So they turned to the East. Suddenly, they discovered that ten thousand Indians were approaching them from the East. They turned to their last avenue of escape, to the West. To their horror, they discovered that ten thousand Indians were also approaching them from the West. As they reined their horses to a stop, the Long Ranger turned to Tonto and asked despairingly, "What are we going to do, Tonto?" Tonto replied, "What do you mean 'we', paleface?"

At times the enemies surrounding us are so great we wonder if we are on the right side. The forces of darkness seem to be superior to the forces of light. Evil men seem to prosper; righteousness seems to go unrewarded. And we wonder if we are on the wrong side.

Such was the attitude that prevailed in the day of Nahum. Judah, God's people, were suffering. Nineveh, which represented the forces opposed to Judah's God, seemed to be succeeding. And the people of Judah wondered if they were on the right side.

Nahum had a word of warning for Nineveh, and indirectly, he spoke a word of consolation to his contemporaries in Judah. Nineveh, Nahum said, which seemed to be so impregnable would be destroyed. "But with an overflowing flood

He will make a complete end of its site, and will pursue His enemies into darkness" (1:8, NASB). The Lord God, Nahum said, who seemed to be ineffective, would eventually exert his authority. "Whatever you devise against the Lord, he will make a complete end ot it" (1:9, NASB).

Nahum proclaimed to the people of his day, mired in pessimism, that although Judah is suffering, and Nineveh is succeeding, the final score is not in yet. God will ultimately bring judgment of a sinful Nineveh, and He will spare a righteous Judah.

That is a message we need in our day, for we, too, sometimes feel that the wrong side is winning. While coaching a baseball team of young boys, I felt that the wrong side was winning at times. In our first game we were behind six runs. As the boys came into the dugout, I tried to exhort them to make a come back. I kept saying, "All right, boys. Don't get pessimistic!" One of the boys asked, "Coach, what does pessimistic mean? Does it mean we think we're going to lose?" That's a prettty good definition of pessimism. It means thinking we are going to lose.

That attitude often invades our lives as it did in the day of Nahum. How we need to hear again the prophet's message of the awesomeness of God.

1. *His Provisions*

To Judah, Nahum declared that God is awesome in his provisions. "The Lord is good," Nahum said, "a stronghold in the day of trouble, and He knows those who take refuge in Him" (1:7, NASB).

A boy wrote home to his father: "Dear Dad: You haven't sent me a check in two weeks. What kind of Christian kindness is that?" His father responded, "Dear Son: That is known as unremitting Christian kindness." God's kindness toward his children is not unremitting, but obvious and abundant in its provisions.

Probably no one has written with more penetrating perception of the provisions of God than has John Claypool in his book, *Tracks of a Fellow Struggler.* At the death of his daughter, Laura Lue, he had to find some answers to the question, "Does religion really make any difference when the bottom drops out?" He found solace and strength in the promise of God in Isaiah 40:30-31. This promise of divine help to man is described in three forms: the ecstasy which enables us at times to "mount up with wings as eagles"; the energy that enables us to "run, and not be weary"; and the endurance that enables us to "walk, and not faint." It was the third form that God's provisions took for the Claypools in their darkness. As he puts it: "When there is no occasion to soar and no place to run, and all you can do is trudge along step by step, to hear of a Help that will enable you 'to walk and not faint' is good news indeed."[35]

To his contemporaries, discouraged by the difficulties of their lives, Nahum proclaimed that God would provide them the strength to see it through. The same God who provided the ecstasy at the crossing of the Red Sea and the energy for the crossing of the Jordan River into the Promised Land, would provide the endurance to see it through until he brought judgment upon Nineveh.

2. *His Punishment*

To Nineveh, Nahum declared that God is awesome in his punishment. "But with an overflowing flood He will make a complete end of its site, and will pursue His enemies into darkness" (1:8, NASB).

The story of Toni Jo Henry was popularized in the sermon "Payday Someday" by R. G. Lee. Toni Jo, a popular night club entertainer, had been sentenced to die for killing a man in a brawl. As she approached the electric chair, she paused to look up at the ceiling. Then she whispered, "I knew all along that God ran the show of his universe; and to think I believed I could steal one little act."

This is the ultimate outcome of the sovereignty of God. God is in charge of the show. This is his world. He created it. He will consummate it. Because God is a holy God, "the Lord will by no means leave the guilty unpunished" (1:3, NASB).

3. *Conclusion*

On the fence at a seminary was a piece of theological graffiti: "God is dead: Nietzche." Someone scratched it out and wrote below it, "Nietzche is dead: God!"

Caught up in the immediacy of the situation, we sometimes begin to doubt the sufficiency and supremacy of God. Take the long look, Nahum suggested, and we will discover that the awfulness of man is no match for the awesomeness of God. Nietzsches and Ninevehs alike will be swept up in the tide of his unfolding purpose. "Hallelujah! For the Lord our God, the Almighty, reigns" (Rev. 19:6*b*).

HABAKKUK

35. Standing Before a Silent God

Habakkuk 1:1-2

A mother was dying in a hospital bed. Her two daughters were by her side. All day the mother had been praying compulsively. As she saw me, she whispered, "I just can't seem to get my prayers past the ceiling."

How many times have we, too, stood before a silent God and wondered why our prayers were not answered? Like Habakkuk we cry out, "Oh, Lord, how long must I call for help before you will listen?" (TLB). Why do our prayers go unanswered?

1. *Something in God's Plan*

A close study of the Bible reveals an amazing insight. Not all of the Bible heroes received affirmative answers to prayers. Some did, and we usually think first of these answered prayers. Abraham's servant prayed for God's direction in finding a wife for Isaac, and God led him to Rebekah (Gen. 24:10-15). Moses, standing before the Red Sea, prayed for God's deliverance, and the water parted to allow the people of Israel to cross over on dry land (Ex. 14:15). Hannah prayed for a son and the result was Samuel (1 Sam. 2). When Elijah prayed for a manifestation of God's power, the fire came down from heaven and consumed the sacrifice (1 Kings 18).

However, alongside those immediately answered prayers of God's saints are some other prayers which "didn't get past the ceiling."

Moses begged God to let him lead his people into the Promised Land. Instead, Moses died on Nebo's peak, his request refused.

Paul prayed three times for the removal of that vexatious

handicap he called his "thorn in the flesh." Instead, he was compelled to make the best of it for the rest of his life.

Even the Master himself in Gethsemane's garden cried out for release from the appalling cup of the cross. Instead, he had to drink it to the dregs.

The Bible is full of unanswered prayers. A close examination of these unanswered prayers will give insight into why some of our prayers are unanswered today. Why was Moses refused the passage into the Promised Land? Why was Paul's thorn not removed? Why did Jesus have to go to the cross? The simple answer is that these prayers were denied so that a far greater purpose in God's kingdom could be served.

Likewise, some of our prayers are unanswered because God has in his plan another alternative which will mean infinitely more to us and his kingdom in the long run.

2. *Selfishness*

Another explanation for unanswered prayer is found in James 4:3. Some prayers are not answered because we ask for selfish purposes. Our prayers are not in the name of Christ nor in accordance with his will. Instead, they are offered in the name of and for the sake of self.

An ancient Greek legend tells of a young man who saw his image reflected in a pool of water. He fell in love with his reflection and pined away in rapture over it. From this legend comes the term *narcissism* which means excessive self-love. Narcissism is a characteristic of our day. "Looking out for number one" is the basic stance of our day. This narcissism has moved into our prayer life and distorted our understanding of the real purpose of prayer.

The object of prayer is that God might be glorified. At times we think of prayer as an Aladdin's lamp which we use to glorify self. Too often our prayers are like that of a young lady who said, "Dear Lord, I'm not just asking for myself but please give my mother a son-in-law!"

Can we not pray for ourselves? Sure, but we should pray for ourselves unselfishly. Unselfish prayer for self is prayer which seeks not comfort but conformity to the will of God. Prayer is not an end in itself but is a means to a greater end which is to glorify God.

3. *Sinfulness*

Isaiah 59:2 indicates yet another reason for unanswered prayer. Our sins cut us off from God. God's arm is not shortened nor has he gone deaf. Instead, our sins have formed barriers which block us off from God's purpose and plan.

In a Catholic church a sign hung over a shrine which said, "This Shrine is out of order. Do not worship here." That is a parable of what sin does to the Christian. It makes us out of order spiritually.

Answered prayers are preceded by genuine confession of sin by which the barriers are broken down so that God's message can get through.

4. *Spitefulness*

Jesus implied in Matthew 5:23-24 that if you are experiencing a strained relationship with another person when you worship, your worship will not be effective. Instead, you should go settle the problem. Then return to worship.

When Leonardo da Vinci was working on his painting, "The Last Supper," he became angry with a certain man. He lashed out at the man with bitter words and threats. Returning to his studio, he attempted to work on the face of Jesus. He could not do it. He was so agitated that he could not compose himself to continue his work. Finally, he put down his tools and sought out the man and asked his forgiveness. The man accepted his apology and Leonardo was able to return to his workshop where he finished painting the face of Jesus.

The point is that you cannot harbor grudges in your heart, you cannot allow the wicked whisper of hatred to sound in your ear, and still receive an answer to your prayer. Prayer and forgiveness go hand in hand. No man can be wrong with his brother and right with God at the same time.

What is the pathway that leads to answered prayer? The shortest route to God is by way of our brothers. As we forgive them and release our spitefulness, we open up the channel of communication to God.

ZEPHANIAH

36. Alumni of the Church

Zephaniah 1:12

The phrase caught my eye recently when a man described himself as "an alumnus of the church." The general term *alumni* connotes past involvement in an organization but present disengagement. An alumnus of the church, then, is a person who was once actively involved in the spiritual community of believers but is no longer. This modern-day description of disengaged Christians is paralleled by the phrase of Zephaniah who described some in his day as "stagnant in spirit."

What causes a person to become an alumnus of the church? What creates the condition of spiritual stagnation?

A recent survey of church alumni revealed four reasons why they had dropped out of the church. Theologically, they were disturbed by the narrow beliefs of the church. Economically, they were turned off by the constant appeal for money. Ethically, they felt restricted by the stringent moral standards the church espoused. Practically, they had become involved in other leisure activities outside the church which consumed their time.

What causes a person to become an alumnus of the church?

1. *Pessimism*

Sometimes spiritual stagnation is the result of a conviction that God is no longer at work in the world.

The "God-is-dead" controversy is now past history. No longer does the theme polarize theologians and headline our weekly news magazines. The experience, however, is still with us. For many people the word "God" is still an empty word. They do not feel God's presence. They do not hear God's proclamations. They do not discern God's purpose. They have given up on God.

A piece of graffiti on a fence suggested: "Go to church and find God." Painted beneath it was the response of a modern-day skeptic: "I went to church, and God was not there."

Most of the alumni of the church, those sometimes saints who have become stagnant in spirit, have lost the sense of God's presence in their lives.

2. *Passivity*

How does this pessimistic conviction arise in the heart of a believer? Usually, a deteriorating faith is the result of the neglect of the disciplines of the Christian life. Instead of active dedication to the patterns that lead to growth, a spirit of passivity leads to indifference and apathy.

Sometimes a person will say, "I quit going to church because I no longer believe in God." Closer to the truth would be the statement, "I quit believing in God because I no longer go to church." Likewise, we could say, "I quit believing in God because I no longer pray," and "I quit believing in God because I no longer study his Word." It is not the loss of faith that results in diminished dedication. It is diminished dedication that leads to loss of faith.

What are the disciplines, neglected by the alumni of the church, which will lead to a rekindling of the fire of faith within? Robert Raines suggests six "grooves of grace" through which spiritual growth can be experienced: corporate worship, daily prayer, Bible reading and study, giving of money, service, and witness. Spiritual growth occurs through a disciplined practice of these grooves of grace. Passivity concerning these practices will result in spiritual stagnation.[36]

3. *Preoccupation*

Take the matter a step further and ask, "Why do we become passive and neglectful concerning these disciples that lead to growth?" The answer is, "We become too preoccupied with other, less important activities."

One of the lessons we most need to learn today is that the

Christian life is a life of selectivity. Most often the choice is not between good and bad but between good and better or between better and best. The Christian life must be an intentional life, a life of choice, a life of positive discrimination. The fact that "Life can be wasted in riotous non-selectivity" was elaborated by Victor Frankl. "Unless a man wishes to drown," Frankl said, "he has to become selective. That is to say, he has to become able to select when to turn on the TV set, when to turn it off, what books and what journals to read and what to throw in the wastebasket. Selectiveness means that we have to be responsible for what is important and what is not, what is essential and what is not, what is valuable and what is not, what is meaningful and what is not. We have to be capable or become capable of such decision making."[37]

"Riotous non-selectivity" is probably the greatest cause of spiritual stagnation today. Paul concentrated on the spiritual. "One thing I do," Paul declared (Phil. 3:13). In contrast, our spiritual involvement gets lost in the shuffle of all the other demands of daily living that we try to fulfill.

Renewal of spirit will occur when we lean to put first things first. "But seek first His kingdom and His righteousness" (Matt. 6:33, NASB). That was the demand of Jesus. Obedience to that command is the first step toward spiritual renewal.

HAGGAI

37. On Leaving God Out

Haggai 1:9

A most unusual advertisement was placed in the newspaper one day. On the front page, in a very conspicuous place, was a notice asking the reader to turn to the back page. When he turned to the back page, the reader found the entire page was empty except for some miniscule printing at the bottom. In the extreme right-hand corner, in very small print, was the sentence: "Is this where you are putting God in your life?"

That was the question Haggai put to the Hebrew people who had returned to their Land of Promise. Under Zerubbabel, about 50,000 Hebrews had returned to the land of Judah. They returned with a renewed commitment to God. That religious zeal was short-lived, however. Soon, indifference and apathy set in.

Haggai was God's spokesman to call the people of Judah to a renewed commitment to God. The essence of Haggai's message is found in our text. Haggai pronounced God's judgment on Judah. Why? "Because of My house which lies desolate, while each of you runs to his own house." Haggai's contemporaries were putting God on the back page of their lives, in the extreme right-hand corner, in very small print!

Where do you put God in your life? Like God's people in Haggai's day, God's people today have left God out of our lives.

1. *Our Relationships*

In an ancient story, a beggar came to a wise old man for some bread and was invited into his tent. As the food was set before them, the old man gave praises to God. The beggar did not—he watched in silence while the man gave thanks.

"Why do you not praise God?" asked the thankful man. "Why should I praise God?" asked the beggar. "What has he done for me? Why has he allowed me to be so poor?" Hearing these words, the host angrily chased the beggar from his tent, beating him with his staff.

When the beggar had gone, God came to the man and said, "Why did you not feed the beggar, and why did you beat him?" "Because," said the self-righteous man, "he would not praise you." God responded, "That man has not praised me for twenty years, and he is still alive. He has not praised me because during all that time you have neglected him. He is alive at all only because I am less religious than you are and have not allowed him to perish. It seems to me, friend, that if I were as religious as you appear to be, there would be no one left alive on the earth!"[38]

Where is God in our relationships? Does his compassion color our attitude toward others? Does his love motivate us to missions of mercy for others? Is the patience with which he relates to us duplicated in our relationships with others? Or do we leave him out of our relationships?

2. *Our Riches*

As a rich patron left the services on a Sunday morning, she asked the pastor if he had seen her new diamond. "Yes," the pastor replied, "I noticed it when you put your twenty-five cents in the offering plate!"

Diamonds for ourselves, and leftovers for God! That is the tragic reality that has emerged in the church today. Like the man who wanted everything to be baptized except his billfold, so we today want to leave God out of our finances. Giving to God, however, is an inescapable dimension of our relationship to him. And it grows out of a proper understanding of our relation to material things.

To whom do all the material possessions of the earth belong? The communists say, "They belong to the workers." The socialists say, "They belong to the state." The capitalists say, "They belong to whoever is strong enough to take them."

The humanists say, "They belong to man." The Bible says, "They belong to God." "The earth is the Lord's, and the fulness thereof; the world, and they that dwell therein" (Ps. 24:1, KJV). God owns all the created order. It belongs to him because he made it.

What then is man's relationship to these material possessions? The answer God gave to Adam and Eve is that we are to be supervisors and developers (Gen. 1:28). In the New Testament, we are called stewards (1 Cor. 4:1). A steward was a manager or an overseer. He did not own the house. He managed the house for someone else to whom he was responsible.

We are developers for God, managers of the world on his behalf, responsible to him for what we do with it. Our accountability before God determines how we earn our money, and how we use our money. When we look at what is God's and say, "It is mine," when we develop what Helmut Thielicke called "the master of the house syndrome," then we have left God out of our riches.

3. *Rejoicing*

As mom and dad were driving down the street, their hearts stopped when they heard the back door open. Their five-year-old son had opened the door. Miraculously, he held onto the arm rest until they could stop the car. Consequently, he was uninjured. That night as the mother was putting her son to bed, she said, "Son, we need to thank God today for saving you when the car door opened." "Why should we thank him?" the boy queried. "I was the one who held on."

How like the attitude we develop toward our blessings in life. We have so much to be thankful for. How often we leave God out of our rejoicing.

Where is God in your life? Is he the front-page headline? Or is he on the back page, in the extreme right-hand corner, in very small print?

ZECHARIAH

38. Return unto Me

Zechariah 1:2-3

The call to repentance is one of the neglected themes of God's Word. Quite often we preach about the love of God which accepts man as he is and helps him to become what he should be. Often we preach about the peace and joy of the abundant life God makes available to us. Recently, many sermons have been preached about the power of the Spirit-filled life. Sunday after Sunday, we sit in our comfortable pews and hear the encouraging, comforting, messages of the benefits of God's blessings in our lives. But the message of God's Word is not all sweetness and comfort. It is not all precious promises and saccharine sweetness. Side by side with the message of God's love is another message, a message of challenge rather than comfort, a demand rather than a delight. This sometimes forgotten and often ignored message of the Scriptures is the message of God's judgment on the sins of man which issues in his call for repentance.

This call to repentance permeates the Word of God. To the Hebrew people in Solomon's day, God said, "If . . . My people who are called by My name humble themselves and pray, and seek My face and turn from their wicked ways, then I will hear from heaven, will forgive their sin, and will heal their land" (2 Chron. 7:13-14, NASB).

When Jesus inaugurated his ministry, he declared, "The time is fulfilled, and the kingdom of God is at hand; repent and believe in the gospel" (Mark 1:15, NASB).

This call to repentance was at the heart of the message of God's prophets to Israel and Judah. Isaiah warned his contemporaries, "Seek the Lord while He may be found; Call upon Him while He is near" (Isa. 55:6, NASB). Jeremiah proclaimed, "Return, faithless Israel," (Jer. 3:12). Ezekiel declared this word from the Lord: "Repent and turn away from your idols, and turn your faces away from all your abominations" (Ezek. 14:6, NASB).

This call to repentance which emanated from the prophets and resounded again from the lips of Jesus was the keynote of Zechariah's message to the people of his day.

According to the inscription in Zechariah 1:1, this prophet spoke God's Word during the second year of Darius. This would be about 520 BC. The first group of exiles had returned to the Land of Promise. God's future loomed large before them. However, neglect had evolved into immorality. God's work had been left unfinished. God's Word had been unheeded. Zechariah emerged as God's spokesman during these difficult days.

Much confusion exists about the prophecy of Zechariah. The book is filled with apocalyptic images and visions. The precise meaning of all these images has been laboriously debated. There can be no mistake, however, about the central message of this prophet of God. The keynote of his prophecy is found in our text: Zechariah called his people to return unto God so that God could return unto them. Repent! That was Zechariah's word from the Lord.

1. *The Meaning of Repentance*

What does it mean to repent? Repentance literally means to think again or to change one's mind or to turn. Repentance is not a permanent state of a man's life. Rather, it is a transition from one state to another. Properly understood, repentance involves two aspects.

Repentance means to *turn from something.* The first phase of repentance is to recognize that you are on the wrong path, to regret the direction in which you are headed, and to decide to turn from it. Study again David's anguished cry in Psalm 51:1-8 and the poignant plea of Isaiah (Isa. 6:5) and you will see this negative aspect of repentance. As one old time revivalist put it, "Repentance means you are so sorry for your meanness that you ain't going to do it anymore!"

Repentance also means to *turn to something*. This is the positive dimension of repentance. Repentance means that, after recognizing your mistakes, you want to redirect your whole being in a new direction and onto a new pathway. Without this positive redirecting of your life toward God's plan, repentance becomes nothing more than morbid, fruitless brooding.

Harry Emerson Fosdick once suggested that there are three kinds of people in the world. There are the proud and self-satisfied, the impenitent who do not even realize the mess they are in. Second, there are the penitent who are so crushed by their contrite self-reproach that they wallow in their self-pity. Then, there are people like the prodigal son (Luke 15) who hate themselves for their failure, but who find in that shame the stimulation to say, "I will rise up and go to my Father."[39]

You have not known the fullness of the experience of repentance until you have moved from the impenitent stage of pride through the penitent stage of self-reproach to the vibrant, exhilirating stage of new life in the power of God.

To repent means to turn from our sin so that we may turn to God.

2. *The Motivation of Repentance*

Why should we repent? What is the motivation for turning from our sin and turning to God?

We must *turn from our sin* because of what sin does to us. Sin has many effects in the life of the sinner, none of which is any more tragic than the estrangement from God which it causes. Sin separates us from God. The Bible declares it (Isa. 59:2); human experience confirms it. Sin creates a barrier which separates us from fellowship with our Father.

Ralph Barton, successful cartoonist, left this note pinned to his pillow as he took his own life: "I have had few difficulties, many friends, great successes; I have gone from wife to wife, and from house to house, visited great countries of the world, but I am fed up with inventing devices to fill up twenty-four hours of the day."[40]

Friends, fame, finances, and even family can never fill the vacuum left by the absence of God. Life comes when God returns to us. God returns to us when the barrier of sin is removed by confession and repentance.

We must *turn to God* because only he can forgive us.

W. A. Criswell tells of a man, in the days of Queen Victoria, who was sentenced to life in prison for a crime he did not commit. A friend on the outside, convinced of his innocence, worked untiringly for his release. Finally, after years of research, the friend found the information he needed. Before Queen Victoria herself, the man made his appeal and won his case. Queen Victoria signed the pardon for the man in prison. With gladness and joy, he went to the prison, entered the cell where his friend had been incarcerated and cried, "Look, I have your pardon. You are a free man. . . . Your pardon has been signed by the queen herself!" Instead of a joyous response, the prisoner lifted his shirt to exhibit a large, ugly, devastating cancer. Gazing into the eyes of his liberator, the prisoner said, "Go ask the Queen if she can heal this."[41]

Sin is a cancer on the soul that leads inevitably to spiritual death. Only God can heal it. If we will return unto him in repentance, he will return unto us in redeeming power.

MALACHI

39. When You Really Worship

Malachi 1:7—2:9

Karl Barth, the eminent German theologian, said, "Christian worship is the most momentous, the most urgent, the most glorious action that can take place in human life." Malachi, the eminent Hebrew prophet, said that worship was so repugnant to God that God wanted someone to close the door of the Temple so that the worship would cease (1:10).

Which is it? Is worship pleasing to God or repugnant to God? The truth is that it can be either. It depends on the attitude and the action of the worshiper.

Worship in Malachi's day had become repugnant to God because of the attitude with which the believers approached worship and because of the abuses into which they had fallen. At least one commentator says that the theme of the Book of Malachi was the desire to call the people back to worthy worship without which there could be no pleasing God and thus no prosperity for his people.

Is worship in our day "the most glorious action that takes place in human life"? Not usually, but it can be. Malachi suggests to us the elements of real worship.

Real worship is:

1. *Worship in Which God Is Honored*

The true purpose of worship is to honor God. This was the declaration of the psalmist: "Come, let us worship and bow down; Let us kneel before the Lord our Maker for He is our God" (Ps. 95:6-7, NASB). The fact that his contemporaries were not honoring God with their worship was the reason for the prophet's condemnation (Mal. 2:2).

The most common Old Testament word for worship is *shachah* which means to have a reverential attitude toward. The basic New Testament word for worship is *proskuneō* which means to "kiss the hand towards one" or to "prostrate oneself before someone." In both cases, the idea of honoring God is primary.

Henry Ward Beecher, pastor of the Plymouth Church in Brooklyn for many years, was one of the most famous preachers in America. One Sunday, while he was gone, he had his brother Tom substitute for him. When Thomas walked to the pulpit, the people realized that Henry Ward Beecher was gone. Many of the sightseers started for the door. Tom said, "May I have your attention. All who came here this morning to worship Henry Ward Beecher may now leave. All who came to worship God may stay."[42]

People come to worship for many reasons: to hear a certain preacher, to watch their children perform, to visit with their friends, to fulfill an obligation, to enhance their business opportunities, or even to see what everyone else is wearing! There is only one acceptable reason for coming to worship and that is to give honor and praise to God.

If you leave a worship service saying with the psalmist, "Great is the Lord, and greatly to be praised," then you have truly worshiped (Ps. 48:1, NASB).

Real worship is:

2. *Worship in Which Man Is Helped*

In worship, man entreats God's favor that he may be gracious unto the worshiper (Mal. 1:9). Worship is not only designed to meet the demand of God but also to meet the need of man.

How is man helped in worship? For man's guilt, worship provides the opportunity for forgiveness. For man's loneliness, worship provides the opportunity for companionship with God. For man's weakness, worship provides the opportunity to tap God's power. For man's anxiety, worship provides the opportunity to experience God's peace. For man's inconsistency, worship provides the discipline that leads to stability.

P. T. Forsythe once said that unless there is within us that which is above us we will soon yield to that which is around us. Worship is the supply channel of God's power.

Worship is not just for God's sake. It is for man's sake as well. "If you leave church with your faith stronger, your hope brighter, your love deeper, your sympathies broadened, your heart purer, and with your will more resolute to do the will of God, then you have truly worshiped!"[43]

Real worship is:

3. *Worship in Which Sacrifice Is Heightened*

One of the signs of the decadence of worship in Malachi's day was the polluted sacrifices which they were offering to God (Mal. 1:13).

Every true worship experience demands a response on the part of the worshiper. If you have been in church but have never been compelled to give sacrificially to the work of God, then you have not truly worshiped. If you have been in a service but have never once felt the compulsion to say with Isaiah, "Here am I. Send me!" (Isa. 6:8), then you have never truly worshiped. Real worship is an encounter with God in which we are compelled to respond in some tangible way to his grace in our lives.

Worship is a central part of the experience of being a Christian. We should worship, not just to pacify our peers or to promote our pastor. We should worship to honor God, to help ourselves grow, and to stimulate our responsiveness to the God whose children we are. That's real worship!

NOTES

Old Testament

1. Charles L. Wallis, ed. *The Minister's Manual*, 1981 Edition (San Francisco: Harper and Row, 1980), p. 245.

2. William Barclay, *The Letter to the Hebrews* (Philadelphia: The Westminster Press, 1955), pp. 161-162.

3. John M. McBain, *It Is Required of Stewards* (Nashville, Tenn.: Broadman Press, 1972), p. 31.

4. Raymond E. Balcomb, *Stir What You've Got* (Nashville, Tenn.: Abingdon Press, 1968), p. 117.

5. Herbert Lockyer, *The Art & Craft of Preaching* (Grand Rapids, Mich.: Baker Book House, 1975), p. 17.

6. W. E. Sangster, *Power in Preaching* (Grand Rapids, Mich.: Baker Book House, 1958), p. 90.

7. Ibid., p. 19.

8. Quoted in Gary Collins, *Overcoming Anxiety* (Santa Anna, Ca.: Vision House Publishers, 1973), p. 146.

9. Bryan Jay Cannon, *Celebrate Yourself: The Secret to a Life of Hope and Joy* (Waco, Tex.: Word Books, 1977), p. 90.

10. R. L. Middleton, *My Cup Runneth Over* (Nashville, Tenn.: Broadman Press, 1960), pp. 9-10.

11. Herbert Lockyer, *The Women of the Bible* (Grand Rapids, Mich.: Zondervan Publishing House, 1967), p. 145.

12. Ralph Conover Lankler, "The Word That Cleanses," in *Pulpit Digest* (May-June, 1981), p. 38.

13. James C. Hefley, *A Dictionary of Illustrations* (Grand Rapids, Mich.: Zondervan Publishing House, 1971), p. 168.

14. D. Elton Trueblood, *While It Is Day* (New York: Harper & Row, 1974), p. 37.

15. Miles J. Stanford, *The Ground of Growth* (Grand Rapids, Mich.: Zondervan Publishing House, 1976), pp. 65-66.

16. *The Los Angeles Times*, June 13, 1981, p. 1.
17. Harold G. Warlick, Jr., *Liberation from Guilt* (Nashville, Tenn.: Broadman Press, 1976), p. 118-119.
18. John M. Drescher, "Empty Chair" in *Pulpit Digest* (May-June, 1981), p. 39.
19. Philip Yancey, *Where Is God When It Hurts?* (Grand Rapids, Mich.: Zondervan Publishing House, 1977), pp. 95-97.
20. Jack Gulledge, "Tears into Rainbows," in *Proclaim* (April-June, 1976), p. 5.
21. William Arthur Ward, "Ward's Words" in *Quote* (July 27, 1975), p. 30.
22. David Mace, *Whom God Hath Joined* (Philadelphia, Penn.: The Westminster Press, 1973), p. 27.
23. Judith Viorst, *Redbook*, February 1975.
24. Jill Morgan, *A Man of the Word* (Grand Rapids, Mich.: Baker Book House, 1972), p. 85.
25. Jerry Clower, *Ain't God Good!* (Waco, Texas: Word, 1975), pp. 160-161.
26. J. Sidlow Baxter, *Explore the Book*, Vol. 3 (Grand Rapids, Mich.: Zondervan Publishing House, 1960), p. 280.
27. Wallis, *The Minister's Manual*, 1981 Edition, p. 238.
28. Harry Emerson Fosdick, *A Great Time to Be Alive* (New York, Harper & Brothers, 1944), p. 220.
29. Wayne Dehoney, *Preaching to Change Lives* (Nashville, Tenn.: Broadman Press, 1974), p. 22.
30. Lyle E. Schaller, *Understanding Tomorrow* (Nashville, Tenn.: Abingdon Press, 1976), pp. 46-49.
31. James Dobson, *What Wives Wish Their Husbands Knew About Women* (Wheaton, Ill.: Tyndale House Publishers, 1979), p. 161.
32. Charles L. Wallis, ed. *The Minister's Manual: Dorah's Nineteen Eighty Edition* (San Francisco: Harper & Row, 1979), p. 263.
33. D. Elton Trueblood, *The Company of the Committed* (New York: Harper & Row, 1961), p. 45.
34. John Havlik, *The Evangelistic Church* (Nashville, Tenn.: Convention Press, 1976), p. 15.
35. John Claypool, *Tracks of a Fellow Struggler: Learning to Handle Grief* (Waco, Tex.: Word Books, 1974), p. 52.
36. Robert A. Raines, *New Life in the Church* (New York: Harper & Row, 1961), p. 59-64.
37. Bruce Larsen, *The Meaning and Mystery of Being Human* (Waco, Tex.: Word Books, 1978), p. 106.
38. Wallis, *The Minister's Manual*, 1981 Edition, p. 249.

39. Fosdick, *A Great Time to Be Alive*, p. 82.

40. A. Dudley Dennison, *Windows, Ladders & Bridges* (Grand Rapids, Mich.: Zondervan Publishing House, 1976), p. 91.

41. W. A. Criswell, *With a Bible in My Hand* (Nashville, Tenn.: Broadman Press, 1978), pp. 24-25.

42. Walter B. Knight, *Three Thousand Illustrations for Christian Service* (Grand Rapids, Mich.: Wm. B. Eerdmans Publishing Co., 1947), p. 742.

43. Franklin M. Segler, *Christian Worship* (Nashville, Tenn.: Broadman Press, 1967), p. 12.

NEW TESTAMENT

MATTHEW

40. What's Right with the Church

Matthew 16:13-19

John Gardner's statement about institutions in the twentieth century being caught in the cross fire between uncritical lovers on the one hand and unloving critics on the other is certainly true of the church.[1] On the one hand are those who see nothing right about the church. On the other hand are those who are blind to the church's problems.

The unloving critics have dominated the scene in recent days. "What's wrong with the church" has become a common topic for modern man. College students debate it. Theologians analyze it. Ministers are perplexed by it. Laymen wonder about it. A negative spirit prevails.

While not ignoring the problems of the church, we need to strike a positive note. The world today needs to hear what is right about the church.

1. *Its Foundation*

Jesus said to Simon Peter in our text: "And I also say to you that you are Peter, and upon this rock I will build *My* church" (v. 18, NASB, author's italics). Jesus did not say that it was Peter's church, or the deacons' church, or the preacher's church. He did not say he would establish the Baptist church or the Methodist church or the Catholic church. He said, "I will build *My* church" (author's italics).

The glory of the church is not that it is labeled with some denominational name. The glory of the church is not that it has a certain preacher in its pulpit or certain affluent people in its membership. The glory of the church is not that it is good or even that it is good enough. The glory of the church is that it is Christ's church! He is the foundation upon which the church is built.

2. *Its Function*

Jesus gave to the church the keys of the kingdom (v. 19). The keys represent authority. Thus, Jesus gave to the church his authority, and left the church with the responsibility to carry out his work. That is the function of the church.

The message that pulsates through the New Testament, the incredible challenge that comes again to the church in every generation, is that the church is the mind through which Christ thinks, the heart through which Christ loves, the voice through which Christ speaks, the hands through which Christ helps, the body of believers through whom Christ works.

The church in every generation has the responsibility to preach the gospel and win the lost and train the disciples and heal the brokenhearted and lift up those who are fallen. That function has been given to nobody else except the church.

3. *Its Fruit*

Jesus gave the keys to the church so that it might liberate people from the bondage of sin and usher them into the kingdom of God (v. 19). Think of the fruit which the early church produced as it carried out its function (Acts 2:41; Acts 4:4; Acts 21:20).

Think of the fruit which the church has produced throughout Christian history. The church in the fourth century produced a Chrysostom. The twelfth-century church produced a Francis of Assisi. The fifteenth-century church produced a Luther. The eighteenth-century church produced a Wesley. The church in our day has produced a Billy Graham, an Elton Trueblood, a Reinhold Niebuhr, and millions of others.

Despite its apparent weakness and evident failures, the church continues to produce the fruit of redeemed men and women who have been liberated from their sins and ushered into the kingdom of God.

4. *Its Fellowship*

When the fruit of redemption was produced in the first century, these new Christians gathered together in the most profound kind of fellowship the world had ever known (Acts 2:44-47). In every generation, the church has provided that same kind of fellowship for those who are in Christ.

There is a relationship-hunger in man that can be met only through shared relationships with others. No fellowship is so binding and lasting as the links of commonality forged between human beings on the basis of a common approach to God through Jesus Christ.

During World War II, some American soldiers took the body of their buddy to a local cemetery. The priest stopped them saying, "You can't bury your friend here if he is not a Catholic." Discouraged but not defeated, the boys buried their fellow soldier just outside the cemetery fence. When they came to pay their respects the next morning, they could not find the grave. They questioned the priest about it, and he said, "The first part of the night I stayed awake disturbed by what I had told you. The second part of the night I spent moving the fence."[2] The fellowship of the church provides a oneness in Christ Jesus that overcomes our individual differences.

5. *Its Future*

Many today declare that we are witnessing the last days of the church. But listen to the resounding declaration of the Master: "Upon this rock I will build My church; and the gates of Hades shall not overpower it" (v. 18, NASB). As the church militant goes out in action for the kingdom of God, there is nothing in the world that can ultimately destroy it. Nothing!

We do not have to apologize about the church. It has Jesus Christ as its foundation. It has the evangelization of the world as its function. It has changed lives for its fruit. It provides a fellowship like no other source in the world. And Jesus said that even if all the forces of evil gather against it, they shall not prevail against his church.

MARK

41. Life-Style in the Kingdom of God

Mark 2:18-20

Jesus was confronted by a question one day concerning his association with sinners and his exuberant spirit. "Why do John's disciples and . . . the Pharisees fast, but Your disciples do not fast?" (v. 18, NASB). In answer to that question, Jesus gave a trilogy of parables which appear together in all three of the Synoptic Gospels. Two of these, the parable of the old and new pieces of cloth and the parable of the old wine in new wineskins, are familiar to us. The first of the trilogy, however, has been largely ignored.

In this parable of the bridegroom and his friends, Jesus gave insight into the life-style of those who were a part of the kingdom of God. The life-style of the Christian was different than that of the Pharisees, a difference reflected in at least three ways.

1. *Liberty*

Life in the kingdom of God was a life of liberty. The question in verse 18 could be paraphrased to say, "Jesus, why are you so different? Why can't you be a good little Jew like everyone else? Why don't you fit the mold?"

An innovator is always a threat to those who are the guardians of the status quo. Man tends to be a stuck-in-the-rut nut. Nowhere is this more obvious than in the area of religious faith. The religion of the Jews in Jesus' day had become crusted with custom and trapped in traditions which forced everyone into a common mold.

When Jesus came to establish the kingdom of God, he announced his purpose was "TO PROCLAIM RELEASE TO THE CAPTIVES" (Luke 4:18, NASB). That included those who were captive to the stifling strictures of the expectations of others. Jesus proclaimed the good news of liberty. The life-style of those in the kingdom of God was not bondage to the traditions of the past, or determination by the expectation of others, but a life of liberty in the Spirit.

2. *Love*

Life in the kingdom of God was also a life of love. The question in verse 18 could be paraphrased to say, "Jesus, why don't you follow the law?"

The religion of Jesus' day was based on the law. It was a negative restrictionism rather than a call to positive righteousness. When Jesus established the kingdom of God, he declared that God was not a Lawgiver whose rigid rules had to be rigorously adhered to but a Father with whom we can experience a living, loving relationship. The basis for our relationship with God is not law but love. Christianity is not a religion but a relationship. Being in the kingdom of God is like getting married. It is a loving relationship with God, new every morning, and fresh to each new generation.

3. *Laughter*

Life in the kingdom of God is also to be a life of laughter. When the Pharisees questioned Jesus in verse 18 they were wondering, *Jesus, why are you so happy*?

Jesus' answer gives insight into the spirit that is to characterize our relationship with God. Jesus compared the kingdom of God to a wedding. Weddings are not times to mourn but times to rejoice. It would be just as out of place for someone who is a part of the kingdom of God to be sad as it would be for a person at a wedding to mourn.

The ingredient most missing in the life of Christians today is that influx of sheer joy which makes living for God as exciting and as enjoyable as being at a wedding. H. L. Mencken once described Puritanism as "the haunting fear that someone somewhere may be happy."[3] That may have been true of Puritanism at its worse, but it is not true of life in the kingdom of God. Life in the kingdom of God brings unparalleled joy because of the benefits that are ours in Christ Jesus.

When you are a part of the kingdom of God, you have *pardon*. Jesus said, "Truly I say to you, all sins shall be forgiven the sons of men" (Mark 3:28, NASB). If you turn in confession to Christ, he will forgive all your sins. No longer will you have to bear the burden of guilt. The realization of that great truth is what makes a Christian happy.

When you are a part of the kingdom of God, you have *purpose*. God has a plan for our world, and as a Christian, you are a part of that plan. When you enter the kingdom of God you become a part of something which is as all-encompassing as eternity, yet so individualized that your part is uniquely significant. The realization of that insight is what makes a Christian happy.

When you are a part of the kingdom of God you have a *presence*. Jesus told His disciples, "It is to your advantage that I go away . . . but if I go, I will send Him (the Helper) to you" (John 16:7, NASB). There is a buddy system in the universe for those who are in the kingdom of God. No matter where you go or what you do, the presence of the Holy Spirit is with you to give strength, stability, and sustenance. The realization of that fantastic promise is what makes a Christian happy.

When you are a part of the kingdom of God you have *permanence*. Paul tells of a day coming when "at the name of Jesus every knee should bow . . . and that every tongue should confess that Jesus Christ is Lord" (Phil. 2:9-10, NASB). When that day comes, we will share his victory. Church buildings are erected and then decay. Church leaders come to the forefront only to be replaced by the saints of the next age. Church programs are produced which soon give way to new programs. But the kingdom of God will last forever. The realization of that priceless privilege is what makes a Christian happy.

Life is different in the kingdom of God. For the Jews of Jesus' day, faith was like a funeral. Jesus said it was like a wedding. Jesus' contemporaries thought of God as an austere

Judge to fear. Jesus said he was like a Father to love. The men of Jesus' time believed that religion was fitting everyone into a mold. Jesus said it was like being let out of a cage. Life in the kingdom of God is a life of liberty, not bondage. It is a life of love, not legalism. It is a life of laughter, not sadness.

LUKE

42. Teach Us to Pray

Luke 11:1-10

Nels Ferré wrote of a Christian convert from Hawaii who spoke about prayer to a seminary in America. "Before the missionaries came to Hawaii," she said, "my people used to sit outside their temples for a long time meditating and preparing themselves before entering. Then they would virtually creep to the altar to offer their petition and afterward would again sit a long time outside, this time to 'breathe life' into their prayers. The Christians, when they came, just got up, uttered a few sentences, said Amen, and were done. For that reason my people called them haolis, 'without breath,' or those who failed to breathe life into their prayers."[4]

Most people believe in prayer. And most of us do pray. However, the greatest need facing all of us is to breathe life and vitality into our prayers. This is the situation in which the disciples found themselves. Their request to Jesus should be our request: "Lord, teach us to pray." In response to their request, Jesus suggested several principles for a vital prayer life.

1. *The Principle of Regularity*

It was "while He was praying in a certain place" (v. 1, NASB), that the disciples came to Jesus with their request. This implies that the disciples had observed in Jesus' life a regular pattern of prayer.

Regularity in prayer is an important principle for us today. This means to pray in a certain place, with a certain purpose, at a certain time. Power in prayer comes to those who discipline themselves to the regular practice of daily prayer.

2. *The Principle of Preparation*

Jesus instructed his disciples to begin with this phrase: "Our

Father who art in heaven, hallowed be Thy name" (Matt. 6:9, NASB). This phrase did not locate God but rather it described God. It reminds us that he is a Heavenly Father, a holy God. Before we can experience power in our prayer, we must have a true awareness of who God is. We must approach him in the right way.

Nels Ferré declares that the two beginning steps of powerful prayer are relaxation and recollection. Relaxation keeps us from rushing thoughtlessly into God's presence. Recollection reminds us with whom we are dealing.[5]

It is not the arithmetic of our prayers that counts (how many they are), nor the rhetoric of our prayers (how eloquent they are), nor the geometry of our prayers (how long they are), nor the logic of our prayers (how convincing they are), nor the method of our prayers (how orderly they are), nor the orthodoxy of our prayers (how sound in doctrine they are). It is the sincerity of our prayers about which God is most concerned. That sincerity comes only as we are properly prepared to come into the presence of a holy God.

3. *The Principle of Inclusiveness*

In the Model Prayer which Jesus gave his disciples, he covered the whole gamut of our needs, both physical and spiritual. The point is that we can pray to God about anything. When a little girl prayed, "God, help Elizabeth's grandmother to get well in her nerves so that she won't go nuts, and Elizabeth won't go nuts with her," I believe God heard her prayer. Everything that is important to you is important to God, and you can talk to him about it.

Andrew Carnegie once asked a friend, "Why should I pray? . . . Name one thing that God can give me that I don't already have." Carnegie's friend replied, "He might give you humility."[6] If you need it, you can talk to God about it.

4. *The Principle of Perseverance*

This is the lesson of the parable in verses five through eight. Perseverance is the key which brings answers to our prayer. This is the lesson of Abraham (Gen. 18:23), of Jacob (Gen.

32:24), of Moses (Deut. 9:25), of Gideon (Judg. 6), and of David (2 Sam. 12:16-18).

Perseverance is the key to power in prayer. Unless we pray like Jacob did until the blessing comes, or like Gideon did until he received the assurance needed, or like Paul and Silas did until the doors of the Philippian jail swung open and released them from their bondage, or like the one hundred and twenty did at Pentecost until the power of God descended on them and transformed them into a mighty spiritual army, that is, until we learn to pray with perseverance, we have not yet learned how to pray.

Hudson Taylor made remarkable gains for Christ in China before communism closed the door to missionaries. Prayer was an important part of his ministry. To find quiet time for uninterrupted prayer, Taylor always rose early in the morning before daylight. He once told a friend that "the sun has never risen upon China without finding me at prayer."[7] That is the kind of persistent prayer that God answers.

5. *The Principle of Faith*

In verse 13, Jesus made a comparison between our willingness to respond to the requests of our children and God's willingness to respond to the requests of his children. If we give to our children, we should have faith to believe that God will also give to us.

Faith is the hand by which we reach out and take to ourselves the things that God has prepared for us. When our prayers are unanswered and we lack the power to win spiritual victories for him, the explanation Jesus will give is the same answer he gave to those first disciples when they could not heal a young boy: "Because of the littleness of your faith" (Matt. 17:20, NASB).

When we learn to pray in faith believing that he will do everything we ask in his name and according to his will, then we have learned how to really pray.

JOHN

43. What Does the Holy Spirit Do?

John 16:7-14

A great deal is being said and written today about the Holy Spirit. This marks a notable change from the situation only a few years ago. After a sermon I preached in my church in the late sixties, one of the young people approached me with a blend of enthusiasm and uncertainty on her face. She confided that this was the first sermon she had ever heard about the Holy Spirit.

A few years ago the Holy Spirit was neglected in our preaching. How different from today! Almost every religious periodical published, almost every book that comes off the press, and almost every religious conference convened has something to say about the Spirit and the Spirit-filled life. A safe conclusion is that never has as much been said about the work of the Holy Spirit as in our day.

This profusion of proclamations about the Holy Spirit has often led to confusion. Clarity is needed in the church today. What better place to go to clarify our thinking on the Holy Spirit than to the Master himself. In his special teaching included in the final chapters of John's Gospel, Jesus had some significant things to say about the Holy Spirit. What does the Holy Spirit do?

1. *Establishes Our Relationship*

The Bible clearly declares that man without Christ is separated from God. "Your iniquities have separated you from God, your sins have hid his face that he may not see" (Isa. 59:2, author's translation). Our sins create a wall that separates us from the One by whom and for whom we were made.

Salvation is that experience in which we are brought back

into a relationship with God. Our sins are removed. The barriers are broken down. The obstacles are swept away. We are reconciled to God. The death of Christ makes this reconciliation possible. As Paul stated it, "God was in Christ reconciling the world to Himself" (2 Cor. 5:19, NASB). It is the death of Jesus that makes this new life possible for us.

But how do we appropriate this new life? How do we enter into this new relationship? That is the work of the Holy Spirit. Ephesians 4:30 (NASB) declares, "Do not grieve the Holy Spirit of God, by whom you were sealed for the day of redemption." Titus 3:5 and 1 Corinthians 6:11 suggest the same idea. This is the impact of what Jesus told the disciples in John 16:8-11. The Holy Spirit convinces us of our need of Christ and draws us to him. He establishes our relationship with Christ, and puts God's stamp of approval on us.

2. *Enriches Our Life*

When the Holy Spirit establishes us in a new relationship with God, he is not through with us. He has only begun. Jesus said, "He shall take of mine, and will disclose it to you" (John 16:14, NASB). The Holy Spirit dwells in the life of the believer to help us experience the abundant life Christ provides.

How does the Holy Spirit enrich our lives? First, by giving us gifts (1 Cor. 12:7). As we develop these gifts and dedicate them to the Lord, our lives will be enriched. Second, by producing certain fruit within us (Gal. 5:22-23). When we allow the Holy Spirit to fill, control, and dominate our life, we will enjoy this fruit. Third, by developing us toward Christlikeness (Eph. 1:13-14). The Holy Spirit helps our new nature win the victory over the old nature which still resides within us.

3. *Enlightens Our Mind*

A specific aspect of this enrichment is what the Holy Spirit does to our mind. Jesus told His disciples that there were many things they could not yet understand (John 16:12). The Holy Spirit, however, would reveal those things to them and guide them into all truth.

One of the most marvelous ministries of the Holy Spirit is

his teaching ministry. A church recently voted to call a man as their "resident theologian." This is what the Holy Spirit is to every believer. He is our resident theologian, guiding and directing our minds to discern the deep things of God.

In John 14:18 Jesus promised the disciples, "I will not leave you as orphans." The Greek word translated "orphans" was often used to speak of students or disciples who were deprived of the presence and teaching of their beloved master or rabbi.[8] The promise, then, is that we will never be without our divine teacher. Every believer has a Master teacher dwelling within, the Spirit of truth. He goes with us everywhere we go, faces every experience we face, confronts every decision we confront, and shows us the way to go.

4. *Encourages Our Heart*

The word *paraclete* which Jesus used to describe the Holy Spirit is translated "Comforter" in the King James Version, and "Helper" in the New American Standard Bible. The word actually means "one called alongside to help." One Greek writer used the word to speak of a general putting fire and courage into dejected troops before they faced a difficult battle.[9] It means to encourage.

Life gets tough sometimes. Someone has suggested that everyone either is a problem, has a problem, or lives with one. Depression and discouragement are familiar companions to us all. The promise of Jesus is that whenever discouragement and depression set in, the Holy Spirit is not just with us but within us to console us, to fill us with courage, to cheer us on, and to keep us going.

5. *Empowers Our Spirit*

Jesus commanded his disciples to go to Jerusalem and wait for the Holy Spirit to come. Attached to the command was a promise. "You shall receive power when the Holy Spirit has come upon you" (Acts 1:8). This promise was fulfilled at Pentecost. Luke described the scene thusly: "And when they had prayed, the place where they had gathered together was shaken, and they were all filled with the Holy Spirit, and began to speak the word of God with boldness" (Acts 4:31).

Paul described the secret of spiritual power in Ephesians 3:16 when he said that we are "strengthened with power through His Spirit in the inner man." This truth is woven through all of Christian history. Whenever lives have been changed, whenever churches have been started, whenever the lost have been saved, whenever Christians have been used, whenever power has been experienced, the explanation has always been a mighty movement of the Holy Spirit.

Trace your personal history and you will discover the same truth. Those moments of real power in our life came when we waited upon, yielded to, and were controlled by God's Holy Spirit. The Holy Spirit empowers us with supernatural strength, enabling us to put into practice the things that Jesus taught.

James Wesberry tells the story of a young Jew who entered an old cathedral in Europe. This was one of the most famous cathedrals in the world. An organ of great value was housed in this old cathedral. The organist who played the instrument had developed an undying affection for the organ. He was the keeper of the keys with total responsibility for the instrument.

The young Jew asked the organist about the organ. The old man's eyes glistened with pride as he explained, "It is the finest in the fatherland, sir." The young man expressed a desire to play the organ but the organist refused. He explained how special the instrument was, declaring that he could not let a stranger play it. The young man persisted until finally the organist surrendered the keys.

As the young man began to play, the anguish of the organist was replaced with unparalleled joy. The music began softly, like a gently blowing breeze, then rose to a high level which sounded like peals of thunder. Then the storm subsided as the thunder was silenced, and the music receded in volume until it was like the breathing of a baby in her mother's arms. The young stranger finished, lowered the lid, locked the organ, and returned the key to the keeper of the keys. Still entranced by the music, the old man asked, "What is your name, young man?" The answer came, "My name is Felix Mendelssohn, sir." With tear-filled eyes the old man said, "To think the master was here, and I almost refused him the key."[10]

The Holy Spirit is the master who wants to play on our lives and bring from them all the melodies and symphonies which God has planted within us. We must not refuse him the key.

ACTS

44. *What Every Person Needs to Know About God*

Acts 17:16-33

As Paul strolled the streets of Athens, which was the commercial, intellectual, cultural, and financial center of the world of his day, he was appalled at the rank immorality and rampant idolatry which dominated the life of the people. He saw questions to be answered. He became aware of needs to be met. So Paul began to share with the Athenians a message that could answer those questions and meet those needs.

What was this message? Read closely the sermon recorded in verses 22-31 and you will discover that Paul's message was a message about God. In the midst of the intellectual confusion, moral depravity, and spiritual paucity, Paul felt that the answer to the Athenians' problems was a clear understanding of God.

The overwhelming need of our day is the same as that of Paul's day. We need someone to stand up before us as Paul did before the Athenians and declare, "You have been worshiping God without knowing who he is, and now I wish to tell you about him." There are certain facts everyone needs to know about God.

1. *An Existing God*

First, every man needs to know that God exists. This was the beginning point of Paul's message. In verse 23, Paul said that the Athenians already believed in divine beings. Paul used this fact as a bridge to the Athenians. "You are right at this point," Paul said, "God does exist."

That is a vital message for our day for atheism is a popular stance among the pseudointellectuals of our day. Eugenia Price has said, "More persons than are willing to admit it live uneasily beneath a row of universal question marks about God."[11] In that kind of situation, we need to proclaim to our world that God is alive. He is the power behind every thought of our brain and every beat of our heart and every breath of our body. He is the element in which we live and move and have our being, the final irreducible and inescapable denominator of our universe.

How do we know? All the available testimony points in that direction. The testimony of nature supports the existence of God, for how else could our world have come into being. The testimony of archaeology supports the existence of God, for in every culture archaeologists have discovered evidence of a belief in God. The testimony of man supports the existence of God, for how else can we explain the knowing mind and the loving heart and the purposive spirit of man. Above all, the testimony of Christ supports the existence of God. All these testimonies combine to give undeniable support to the first point of Paul's great message about God. He is an existing God.

2. *An Eminent God*

Every man needs to know of the greatness of God. Paul added this second point to his message in verses 24-26. God is a great God!

God is so great that in his presence all other lights seem to be mere darkness in comparison. He is greater in wisdom than the combined knowledge of a billion Einsteins. He is greater in power than all the atomic arsenals of all the nations of the world. He is greater in authority than all the kings who have ever ruled. He is greater in size than the universe which is itself so big that adequate instruments or proper terminology with which to measure it are not available. He is greater in love than the longings of a million mothers' hearts. This God who exists, Paul said, is a great God.

3. *An Embracing God*

Every man needs to know that God loves him. This is what Paul said in verse 27: "He is not far from each one of us." Paul added that God's purpose in creating the world was that man might find him.

What a message! This God who existed before all the universe as we know it, this God who is eminent among all the powers of our world, is a God who cares enough to come to us and embrace us. God loves us!

The message of God's love is the greatest message of the Bible. It is so great that Paul made it the passion of his life. It is so great that when Augustine discovered it, all the darkness of doubt vanished away, and his life was completely changed. It is so great that when John Newton experienced its reality, he left his slave boats and his carnal life and became a preacher whose total efforts were committed to this theme: "Amazing grace! how sweet the sound, That saved a wretch like me! I once was lost, but now am found, Was blind, but now I see." The message of God's love is so great that when Pascal discovered it, he wrote the message down and sewed it into the lining of his coat, so that he would be constantly reminded that the God of Abraham and Isaac and Jacob is a God who loves us.

God is a God of love, a God whose grace will embrace our lives so that in him we can live, and move, and have our being.

4. *An Exacting God*

In verses 30-31, Paul added yet another dimension of God when he declared that God makes a demand on our lives. What does God demand? He demands a choice. He presents to us the gift of salvation. He reveals his love to us. Then he demands that we respond one way or another to it. Either we accept his gift in Christ, or we reject it. God demands that choice. Every man needs to know that he must decide what he will do with God.

Dr. Wilbur Chapman, preeminent pulpiteer of the past, was confronted one morning after the worship service by one of his deacons. Aware of Dr. Chapman's poor health, he said, "Pastor, I wish you could enjoy the good health that I have. I never have an ache. I never need a doctor. I take no medicine. I am the picture of perfect health."

Three weeks later Dr. Chapman was disturbed by the early morning ring of the telephone. He was asked to come quickly to the home of the deacon mentioned above. Dr. Chapman was met at the door by the man's daughter with tears in her eyes. "This morning," she said, "Dad asked me to meet him in the breakfast room in fifteen minutes. When I dressed, I went and waited for him. After a few minutes' wait, I went to his bedroom to check on him. He was sitting in his favorite chair, with the morning paper in his lap, and his head fallen to his chest. And he was dead!"

Never an ache. Never a pain. Never the need for a doctor. Never the desire for any medicine. He was the picture of perfect health. Yet, in fifteen minutes he had gone out to meet God.[12]

Everyone needs to know that someday he too must stand before God to give an account for his life. By receiving Christ as Savior, every person can be ready for that day.

ROMANS

45. A New You

Romans 8

Bertha Adams was a pitiful case. At seventy-one years of age, she weighed only fifty pounds. She begged door-to-door for food and clothed her emaciated body in Salvation Army clothing. On April 5, 1975, she died of malnutrition in West Palm Beach, Florida, after spending the last few days of her life in a nursing home. When she died, however, authorities discovered that she left behind a fortune of over one million dollars, including more than eight hundred thousand dollars in cash, and several hundred shares of valuable stock which she had stored in two safety deposit boxes.[13]

To think about the wealth she had at her disposal, to consider what she could have enjoyed, and then to see the way she wasted away until there was no more life in her body will lead a person to exclaim, "What a fool she was!"

There are Christians who are just as big of fools, for many of us go through life in spiritual poverty when the Bible declares that we are joint heirs with Christ to all of the riches of God. Listen to what can be ours in Christ Jesus.

1. *A New Position*

Of the problems that plague us, one of the greatest is guilt. It is an agelong problem. Why did Adam and Eve hide behind the tree when God walked in the garden in the cool of the day? The answer is their guilt. Why did King David, the magnificent monarch, fall to his knees with a broken heart? The answer is his guilt. Why did Simon Peter, the bold believer, slip silently off into the darkness to weep? The answer is his guilt. Why did Ananias and Saphira fall dead at the condemnation of Simon Peter? It is because of their guilt. Guilt is a universal human problem.

But listen to what Paul said about those who are in Christ. The scene is the courtroom. The defendant is you. The prosecuting attorney is the law you have broken. The defense attorney is Christ. The judge is God himself. And the decision that comes ringing forth is, "Not guilty." There is no longer any condemnation for those in Christ Jesus (v. 1). We are in a new position before God because of Christ.

2. *A New Potential*

Will Rogers used to say that man was made a little lower than the angels, and he has been getting lower ever since. Who can peruse the daily newspapers and not admit the truth of that evaluation? The natural inclination of man is toward darkness, toward death.

Paul said that in Christ we can change that direction. Jesus not only gives us a new position before God but he also plants within us a new inclination toward life, a potential for growth and development and maturity.

We often speak of salvation as if it were a once-for-all event. Not so. Conversion is an event, a moment when we are given a new standing before God. Salvation is a process that lasts throughout life and takes us from one level of glory to another (2 Cor. 3:18). As birth is not all there is to life, as a foundation is not all there is to a house, as a wedding is not all there is to marriage, so conversion is not all there is to salvation. With the new position comes a new potential.

3. *A New Power*

In addition to a new potential, Christ provides the power to realize that potential. The resurrection power which raised Christ from the dead is also available to us as Christians (v. 11).

Have you ever noticed the contrasting pictures of Romans 7 and Romans 8? In Romans 7 we see a spiritually defeated person crying, "Who will set me free from the body of this death?" (v. 24). In Romans 8 we see a spiritually victorious person declaring, "But in all these things we overwhelmingly conquer through Him who loved us" (v. 37, NASB). What's the difference? The difference is the power which comes when we yield to the Holy Spirit in our lives.

Jesus not only gives us a new potential for growth. He gives us the energy to realize that potential. He not only gives us another chance but he also provides the power to make something of that second chance.

4. *A New Perspective*

In the midst of the "sufferings of this present time" (v. 18), Jesus gives us a new point of view. Life for the Christian is not without suffering or without setbacks. Suffering is a part of the fabric of life for all of us. However, in the midst of suffering, two perceptions enable us to make it through.

In verse 28 Paul declared that the Christian can handle suffering because he knows God will weave all of our hurts and problems into a pattern which will eventually work out into something good. We know that God is in charge of the present, so we can keep going.

In verse 18 Paul declared that the Christian can handle suffering because he knows that the present suffering does not compare with the things God has prepared for us. We know that God is in charge of the future, so we can keep going.

5. *A New Permanence*

Paul listed all of the things that threatened man in verses 31-33. Then he concluded that nothing could ever separate us from God's love in Christ.

At PraiSing 1975 in Nashville, George Beverly Shea was one of the featured artists. Before singing one evening he shared some experiences. He pointed out how frequently original compositions are sent to him with a request for him to record them. One song sent to him was entitled, "God's Grip Don't Slip." That's atrocious grammar, but terrific theology. Once we place our life in God's hand, his grip will never slip. He gives us permanence in our spiritual dimension.

What a chapter Romans 8 is. It's no wonder that D. L. Moody used to say that he would rather live in Romans 8 than in the Garden of Eden. These promises are for us. To claim them today will enable us to be transformed into the new person God wants us to be.

1 CORINTHIANS

46. Understanding Spiritual Gifts

1 Corinthians 12

"I do not want you to be uninformed concerning spiritual gifts. . . ." (v. 1, author's translation). Paul's statement is as relevant to the church today as it was to the church of his day, for there is no element in the church's life about which there is as much confusion as there is about spiritual gifts.

Do I have a spiritual gift? Where do the gifts come from? Why do we have gifts? How do we discover them? These are questions which demand answers. Paul gave some answers in 1 Corinthians 12, for this text is the most exhaustive passage in the New Testament concerning spiritual gifts.

1. *The Distribution of the Gifts*

In verse 7 Paul said, "To each is given the manifestation of the Spirit." This basic statement is reinforced by every other discussion of spiritual gifts in the New Testament. In Ephesians 4:7 (NASB), Paul stated, "But to each one of us grace was given according to the measure of Christ's gift." In his first epistle, Peter declared that each Christian has received a gift (1 Pet. 4:10). In the first letter to the Corinthians, Paul said, "But each has his own special gift from God" (1 Cor. 7:7). The gifts of the Spirit are distributed to every believer.

This rules out self-pity and self-depreciation in the body of Christ. No one can say, "There is nothing I can do for God." Neither can a person say, "I am worth nothing to God." To every Christian the Holy Spirit has given a gift (v. 4). For every Christian the Holy Spirit has chosen a ministry in which to use that gift (v. 5). To every Christian the Holy Spirit has provided the power to carry out that ministry (v. 6). The gifts of the Spirit are distributed to every believer.

2. *The Diversity of the Gifts*

Everyone has a gift, but the gifts of each individual Christian are different. "Now there are varieties of gifts," Paul said in verse 4. These spiritual gifts are distributed individually to the believers as the Holy Spirit wills (v. 11). As there are many parts in the physical body, so are there many parts in the body of Christ (v. 20).

All Christians are gifted by the Holy Spirit. But the Bible makes it very clear that these gifts are distributed to the believer in a rich diversity. That means there is no all-Christian gift, a single gift that every Christian should solicit. Neither is there an all-gift Christian, one who is endowed with all the spiritual gifts. Each Christian is gifted differently according to the plan and purpose of God.

The listing of these spiritual gifts in 1 Corinthians 12:8-10,28-30, and Romans 12:6-8, and Ephesians 4:11, and 1 Peter 4:11 are not exhaustive or exclusive lists. Rather, these lists are illustrative of the variety of gifts given to different Christians.

The diversity with which the gifts are distributed rules out self-sufficiency and self-pride in the body of Christ. No one can say, "I can make it alone." Neither can a Christian claim his gift to be superior to those of other Christians. Every believer has been given a gift which is vital to the ongoing of God's kingdom.

3. *The Demand of the Gifts*

Why does the Holy Spirit endow believers with these spiritual gifts? These gifts are not an adornment for private benefit or an award for distinguished service but an anointment for service. The Bible says, "As each has received a special gift, employ it" (1 Pet. 4:10, NASB). The presence of these gifts in our lives is not a privilege but a responsibility.

Why does the Spirit distribute gifts to the believers? Paul cited three reasons: to produce growth in the church (1 Cor. 12:7; 1 Cor. 14:12), to produce unity within the church (1 Cor. 12:24-25), and to extend the ministry and witness of the church (Eph. 4:11-12). When the Holy Spirit gives these gifts to the believer, they are to be used for the building up of the church, for the strengthening of the fellowship, and for the effective evangelization of a lost and dying world.

4. *The Discovery of the Gifts*

If every Christian has been given a gift, and if these gifts are to be used for the significant purposes just listed, another matter of extreme importance is the discovery of the gifts. How can we know what our spiritual gift is?

The first step is *acceptance*. Believing that you have a spiritual gift is the first step in discovering what it is. Many Christians never discover their gift because they don't believe they have one.

The second step is *awareness*. Study the lists of gifts in the New Testament. These lists are illustrative of the way the Spirit works. Analyze ways in which God has gifted people in the past. Become aware of what these gifts are.

The third step is *appeal*. What do you enjoy doing? What do you do well? What appeals to your concern and motivates you to action? That might be God leading you to the discovery of your gift.

The fourth step is *asking*. James tells us, "You have not because you ask not" (Jas. 4:2, author's translation). Prayer is a key tool in discovering the will and purpose of God. Ask God to show you what your gifts are.

The fifth step is *association*. In our association with others, our Christian friends will often find a cue in our lives, and draw it out, and in so doing help us to find our gift.

One pastor asked a Sunday School teacher to help him counsel some young couples. As she did, the pastor helped her to discover her gift in this area. Consequently, she enrolled in a therapy course. Two years later she was asked to join the hospital staff where she used her gift of counseling. She discovered her gift through association with other Christians.[14]

The sixth step is *action*. Don't get caught in the paralysis of analysis. Do not remain in the passive voice until you discover your gift. Go through the open doors God has set before you. Act on the basis of what you know. Quite often, as we minister to others in Christian love, our spiritual gifts will become clear to us.

5. *The Dedication of the Gifts*

All that Paul said about spiritual gifts in 1 Corinthians 12 leads finally to the point of commitment. To young Timothy, Paul wrote, "I remind you to stir up the gift of God that is within you" (2 Tim. 1:6, author's translation). This challenge comes to us all. Stir up that gift which is within you, and dedicate it to the service of God through your church. Then your church can come alive!

2 CORINTHIANS

47. God's Unspeakable Gift

2 Corinthians 9:15

A wealthy Easterner wanted to outdo his Texas cousin in sending a gift to their grandmother. He purchased a zirkah bird that could speak five languages and sing three operatic arias. He paid $25,000 for the unique animal and sent it to his grandmother. The day after Christmas he called her. "Grandmother," he asked, "how did you like the zirkah bird?" "It was delicious," she responded.

How often gifts are misunderstood! It was also true of the greatest gift, God's gift of his Son. The words available to Paul were not adequate to express the greatness of Christ. So he coined a word that the King James Version translates as *unspeakable*. Jesus is God's "unspeakable gift." The dimensions of this special gift of God are revealed in the New Testament. Several aspects of this "unspeakable gift" need to constantly be clarified.

1. *An Unmerited Gift*

The New Testament unanimously proclaimed that man did not deserve the gift God gave in Jesus Christ. God's love is activated not by our goodness but by our need; not by our spiritual depth but by our spiritual depravity. His action in history to redeem sinful man was not initiated by our loveliness but by his love. God's love came to us when we did not deserve it, before we could ever possibly hope to earn it, and it opens up to us the possibility of new life.

A bashful young man stood in front of the house where his sweetheart lived. He finally mustered the courage to ring the doorbell. When she opened the door he handed her a dozen roses. She was so excited that she grabbed him, kissing him all over the face. He broke away from her and started running away. She cried out, "Johnny, don't leave. I didn't mean to scare you." "You didn't scare me," he responded. "I'm just going to get some more flowers."

You don't have to bring flowers to God to win his love. God loved us before we deserved it. "But God showed his great love for us by sending Christ to die for us while we were yet sinners" (Rom. 5:8, TLB). God's gift of love in Christ is unmerited.

2. *An Unprejudiced Gift*

The qualifications for accepting this love gift from God are the same for every person. As one man has said it, "The ground is wondrously level at the foot of the cross."

This does not mean that the obstacles which must be overcome to receive God's gift of love are always the same. The rich young ruler had to overcome his love for money (Matt. 19). The woman caught in adultery had to overcome her guilt (John 8). The woman at the well at Sychar had to overcome her love for pleasure (John 4). Paul had to overcome his religious pride. Different obstacles prevent individuals from receiving this gift.

Neither does this mean that the same experience is necessary to receive this gift. A man sought counsel for his spiritual problems. One friend said, "Hold on. When I was saved, I really had to hold on." Another suggested, "Let go. When I was converted, I had to let go." Still another counseled, "Look for the light. When I became a Christian, I saw a beautiful blue light." The man later explained that by trying to hold on, let go, and look for the light, he almost missed being saved.

Regardless of the outward form your decision takes and regardless of the obstacles that stand in the way, this gift makes the same demand on every person. That demand is simply to follow Jesus Christ, to turn your life over to him. That is the only way you can become his disciple.

3. *An Unparalleled Gift*

The gift of salvation in Jesus Christ has no counterpart or

equal in history. It is unparalleled.

No other religion has *a risen Savior*. All other religion leaders are still in their tomb. Jesus, however, left nothing behind but an empty tomb and a glorious chorus of angels singing, "He has risen; He is not here; behold, here is the place where they laid Him" (Mark 16:6, NASB).

No other religion has *a perfect Lord*. Into the lives of all the great religious leaders of the world sin came. Imperfections were noted. Yet no blemish was ever detected in Jesus. The thief with a keen eye for wickedness could find no fault in him. The witnesses who were bent on his destruction could find no fault in him. The cold-blooded Roman soldier who nailed him to the cross could find no fault in him. His most intimate companions could find no blemish on his life. He was the One "altogether lovely."

No other religion has *a loving God* who seeks man. In other religions the direction is always from man to God. The God of Christianity, on the other hand, is a God who seeks man.

No other religion provides *a living personality* who helps meet the needs of day-by-day living. God's promise to the first disciples comes to disciples of all ages: "Lo, I am with you alway, even unto the end of the world" (Matt. 28:20).

L. Nelson Bell recounted a story told by a Chinese pastor. He told of a man who fell into a dark, slimy pit. He tried to climb out but could not. Confucious came along, saw the man, and said, "Poor fellow. If he had listened to me, he would never have fallen in." And Confucious walked away. Then Buddha came along. "Poor fellow," said Buddha, "If he'd come up here, I'd help him." He, too, walked on. Then Jesus came by. Seeing the man, Jesus said, "Poor fellow," and then He jumped down into the pit and lifted him out."[15]

Other religions offer rules and regulations, guidelines to follow, and doctrines to believe. Christianity offers a living personality who comes to where we are and lifts us out of the pit.

4. *An Uncontainable Gift*

When a person is right with God and in touch with this unspeakable gift, he will not be able to be quiet about it. The motivation to witness is not something we conjure up from within ourselves. Instead, it comes from a living, dynamic relationship with Christ. As we spontaneously share with others the exciting things happening in our lives, even so a close relationship with Christ will result in the spontaneous sharing of him with others.

5. *An Unending Gift*

There is a permanence about the gift of salvation that comes through Christ. God's gift is not for this world only but for the next world as well. It is not only good for life but also for death.

As Dwight L. Moody moved toward the end of his life, he told a congregation that someday they would hear the news that Moody was dead. "Don't you believe it," he said. "On that day I'll be more alive than I have ever been!" This promise which Jesus gave to Martha, comes to every believer, "I am the resurrection and the life; he who believes in Me shall live even if he dies, and everyone who lives and believes in Me shall never die" (John 11:25-26).

There is no other gift in all the world like the gift God gave to us in Jesus Christ. It is no wonder Paul exclaimed, "Thanks be unto God for his unspeakable gift."

GALATIANS

48. The Price Tags of Freedom

Galatians 5:1

In 1833, the British Parliament voted to abolish the institution of slavery in the Crown Colony of Jamaica. The date set for the emancipation proclamation to go into effect was awaited with growing anticipation by the people. On the night before the glorious day, the slaves did not sleep. Instead, they dressed in their most beautiful clothes and began streaming up the mountainsides to catch the first glimpse of the dawning of their day of freedom. As the first rays of the sun streaked across the horizon, the slaves erupted in irrepressible ecstasy. On that day a Negro spiritual was born which became the theme song for the Civil Rights Movement in our day:

Free at last,
Free at last,
Thank God almighty,
Free at last![16]

The desire for freedom is at the heart of the American spirit. It was the desire for freedom which brought the first colonists to our shores. The Pilgrim fathers, stifled by the religious and political powers of the British Empire, longed for the privilege to define their own existence and shape their own destiny. They braved uncharted seas to come to America where they could experience true freedom.

Our nation was founded upon the idea of freedom. The Constitution of the United States declares that the motivation of the establishment of the United States was the desire to "secure the blessings of liberty to ourselves and our posterity." As Abraham Lincoln expressed it in his address at Gettysburg, our nation was "conceived in liberty."

Freedom has been the watchword of America from the beginning. We have pledged ourselves to the establishment of freedom, fought for the protection of freedom, marched for the recognition of freedom, and prayed for the maintenance of freedom. Freedom and America are synonymous terms.

Freedom is also the watchword of Paul's letter to the Galatian Christians. One commentator calls the book "The Magna Carta of Christian Liberty."[17] In Paul's discussion of Christian freedom, he gave some keen insights which can be applied to freedom in America today. Paul suggested that freedom is never free. In our text, he explained the price tags of freedom.

1. *Commitment*

What does freedom cost? The first answer is commitment. It is Christ who sets us free. There is no freedom apart from commitment to Christ who puts us in a right relationship with God. We know that is true of individuals. It is also true of nations. The secret of America's greatness has been our commitment to God. This commitment to God, which is at the foundation of our nation, is reflected in the motto which adorns our coins: "In God we trust."

Following the Civil War, Salmon P. Chase, secretary of the treasury, received appeals from many people to honor God in some suitable manner on our coins. He instructed the director of the mint to come up with a motto which expressed our dependence on God. Several different mottos were tried before the phrase "In God we trust" gained wide favor. This motto was printed on all United States coins. When the eagle and double eagle of new design appeared in 1907, the motto was omitted. There was such a great outcry that Congress passed an act on May 18, 1908, requiring the motto to appear on all coins issued thereafter.

Every time we look at a coin it is a reminder that there will be no freedom in the long run without an acknowledgement of our dependence on God and our commitment to him. A nation's safeguard is not its culture or Greece would not have fallen, not its political power or Rome would not have fallen. A nation's safeguard is in its righteousness, and that grows out of a commitment to a righteous God. There is no freedom apart from commitment to God. That is the price tag of freedom.

2. *Consistency*

What is the cost of freedom? A second price tag Paul mentioned is consistency. Paul said to the Galatians, "Keep standing firm!" Freedom is not something which, once obtained, is automatically ours forever. Instead, freedom must be maintained by a daily dedication and a dogged determination to fight for and hold on to the freedoms that have been obtained.

During the dark days of World War II, Winston Churchill was invited to return to Harrow, the preparatory school he attended as a boy. The headmaster told the students to listen closely to the words of the world famous statesmen. When Churchill stood before the students, this was his speech: "Never give in. Never give in. Never! Never! Never!" Then he sat down.[18]

We must consistently work at maintaining our freedom, or we will lose it. That is the price tag of freedom.

3. *Caution*

What does freedom cost? Paul gave a third suggestion when he urged caution. "Do not be subject again," Paul said, "to a yoke of slavery." The Greek word translated "subject to" means "ensnared" or "trapped." The reason we must never give up in our quest for freedom is that tyranny never gives up in its quest to take our freedom away. Eternal caution must be maintained to avoid falling into those traps which would take our freedom away. Several enemies stand ready to take our freedom away today.

The tendency to stress rights over responsibilities is an enemy that threatens to dissolve our freedom. A fifth-grade math teacher in Vermont was suspended for two weeks without pay for spanking a student. The student used foul language and obscene gestures, so the teacher turned the boy over her knee and spanked him. At the hearing, one of the members of the board asked her, "Do you not think that the children have rights?" She responded, "It seems like many of these children have more rights than responsibilities."

That is a commentary on our day. A nation which refuses to accept its responsibilities but is always focusing on its rights is not free. Instead, it is bound by its own selfishness.

Indifference is another threat to freedom. Someone has pointed out that thirteen of the last fifteen presidents were elected by a fewer number than the number of qualified voters who stayed at home. That, too, is a frightening commentary on the apathy and indifference of our day. When we do not care enough to get involved in exercising our freedoms, those freedoms will soon be taken away.

Yet another threat to freedom is the desire for security. History is marked with those people who gave away their freedom in return for comfort and security. This is what happened to Israel. Caught in the bondage of Egyptian slavery, freedom was their heart's desire. But the moment they were delivered from the tyranny of Egypt, they were confronted by the complexity of their newfound freedom. Consequently, some wished that they were back in Egypt! Some of the same ones who cried, "Give me liberty or give me death" were now singing a new song: "Give me security, and you can have the agony of freedom."

Both internal and external forces constantly conspire to take our freedom away. That is why Paul urged caution. That is the price tag of freedom.

At the close of the Constitutional Convention in 1787, Benjamin Franklin reportedly said, "We have given you a republic—if you can keep it."[19] That is the challenge to each new generation of Americans. Are we willing to pay the price tags of freedom: commitment, consistency, and caution?

EPHESIANS

49. *Is Your Difference Showing?*

Ephesians 4:17-20

Modern painters can be divided into five categories: those who paint what they see, those who think they paint what they see, those who paint what they think they see, those who think they paint what they think they see, those who think they paint.

People can be divided into three categories: those who think, those who think they think, and those who would rather die than think.

According to one man there are three different age categories in life: youth, middle age, and "my but you're looking well."

Categorizing is a favorite pastime today. We have categories for everything. Paul declared in our text that there is a very simple way to classify all men: those who are Christians and those who are not Christians. Those are the only two categories. Paul further stated that a distinct difference exists between these two categories of people.

The source of this difference is a Christian's commitment to Christ. A Christian has a new commitment in his life. The basic commitment is not to gratify self but to glorify Christ. Christ calls the shots in a Christian's life. He is in charge. Because of that, some noticeable differences will exist between a Christian and one who has not made this commitment to Christ.

But how is this difference to manifest itself? That is where the debate arises. Granted that Christians are to be different from those who are not Christians, how are we to be different?

Some feel the difference should be reflected in our relationship with life in general. This idea spawned the monastic movement of the Middle Ages. Because life is evil and the world is bad, the Christian is to show his difference by completely withdrawing from the world, so the argument went. In fact the more painful you could make life on this earth, the more pious you were. The extremes to which this idea led some saints is almost beyond comprehension.

One monk, Besarion, would not yield to his body's desire for restful sleep, and for forty years he would not lie down while sleeping. Macarius the Younger sat naked in a swamp for six months until mosquito bites made him look like a victim of leprosy. Simeon Stylites spent thirty years on the top of a sixty-foot pillar, and for his deep commitment was exalted to sainthood in the church. In each case, one's dedication was reflected in a total separation from any pleasure of life. Paul warned against such extremes in his letter to the Colossians (2:20-23).

At other times, people have felt that the difference should be reflected in our language. Because you are a Christian, you talk differently. A little boy on a farm illustrated this concept of Christianty. One day the pastor came to visit and was sitting in the living room visiting with the boy's mother. The preacher was seated in a corner chair, so the boy did not see him as he came running into the room with a rat by the tail. The boy said, "Mama, I found this rat and I hit him with a board, and then I threw him against the barn, and then I kicked him, and then I stomped him . . ." At that moment, the boy caught a glimpse of the preacher, so he turned to the preacher and continued, "And then, Pastor, the Lord called him home!"

Others think that the difference is to be reflected in our outward appearance. There are religious groups in America which still dress in a unique way to exhibit their Christian faith. Many Christians have felt at times that it was a sin to wear makeup. Other churches argue about women should wear pant suits to church. In each case, the difference is outward. Jesus suggested that it is not what's on the outside that counts, but what is in the heart (Matt. 12:34).

If the difference is not to be shown by withdrawing from the world, or by talking in a certain way, or by dressing in a certain way, how then is the difference to be shown? Paul gave some suggestions in context.

1. *Think Differently*

Paul suggested that Christians are to think differently. Notice how he described those who do not know Jesus Christ. He said they walk "in the futility of their mind." That is, their minds are filled with empty things. Then, he added that they are "darkened in their understanding." He also referred to "the ignorance that is in them."

Now, let me translate that for you into today's English. Those who do not know Jesus Christ focus all their attention on the material as over against the spiritual, on the temporal as over against the eternal.

The Christian, on the other hand, although he lives in a material world, recognizes another dimension, the spiritual dimension, which is so much more important. The Christian does not concentrate all his attention on the things of this world because he knows they are temporary, they will not last, they are here today and gone tomorrow. Because his eyes have been opened by Jesus Christ, he thinks on spiritual eternal things. His thinking is different.

2. *Feel Differently*

Because the Christian thinks differently, Paul added that he also feels differently. Notice again how Paul described those who do not know Jesus Christ. He referred to "the hardness of their heart" and suggested that they have become callous. Because the non-Christian thinks only on material and temporal things, because his thoughts are only on himself, his heart becomes hardened toward others and he is no longer able to feel compassion for them.

The Christian is different. Because he thinks differently

about life, his attention is focused not on himself but on others. Therefore, he is sensitive to the needs of people and feels a deep compassion for them.

3. *Act Differently*

Because the Christian thinks differently and feels differently, he therefore will act differently. According to Paul, those who do not know Jesus Christ have "given themselves over to sensuality, for the practice of every kind of impurity with greediness."

But the Christian is different. Because he thinks differently and feels differently he will not give himself over to every king of impurity with greediness, but rather he will "put on the new self, which in the likeness of God has been created in righteousness and holiness of the truth."

Mother Theresa is a beautiful example of Paul's argument. Mother Theresa was given a Nobel prize for her work among the poor and outcast. What was the secret of her distinctiveness? It started in her mind. Because her mind was focused on eternal values, she was moved with compassion for the needs of her fellow human beings, and therefore she gave her life in service to them. She thought differently. She felt differently. Therefore, she acted differently.

When you are a follower of Jesus Christ, you too are to be different in those same ways. Is your difference showing?

PHILIPPIANS

50. Principles Of Greatness

Philippians 3:13-14

What an amazing man Paul was! And what an excellent example to emulate! John Henry Jowett, the outstanding English pulpiteer, once said, "If ever mortal man had the key to the house I want opened, Paul does."[20] If ever a man lived the victorious Christian life, Paul was that man.

How did he do it? What were the principles that led him to greatness? No more concise summation of the key principles of his life are found than in our text in the Philippian letter.

1. *Concentration*

"This one thing I do," Paul said in verse 13. *The Living Bible* makes this idea even more vivid: "I am bringing all my energies to bear on one thing." The first principle that led Paul to greatness was concentration.

Because of Paul's consuming concentration on Christ, people would describe him as a fanatic. A fanatic is a person who will not change his mind and will not change the subject. That was Paul. There was one subject about which he talked, one desire by which he was motivated, one purpose for which he lived and that was to magnify Jesus Christ. Paul concentrated all of his energies on this central purpose. That was the secret of his life.

The reason for ineffectiveness in Christian living today is not a lack of love or a lack of desire. It is a lack of concentration. Our time and energy and money and interests are diverted into so many directions that God is lost in the shuffle.

An outstanding concert violinist found her energies consumed by peripheral matters. The violin received the tail end of her day, or was neglected altogether. Success came when she made the decision to concentrate. "I deliberately planned to neglect everything else," she said, "until my practice period was completed. That program of planned neglect accounts for my success."[21]

Planned neglect of peripheral matters allows concentration on the priority matters. So it was with Paul. He selectively concentrated his attention on Christ. That was a key to his success.

2. *Cancellation*

One of the ways Paul concentrated on the present was by "forgetting what lies behind" (v. 13). Paul canceled out of his mind anything in the past which would hinder his spiritual progress in the present. He knew how to forget.

Many are not able to attain greatness in today's living because they carry too many burdens from yesterday. The secret to success is to learn how to forget.

We need to forget our *accomplishments* of the past. To be so enamored with what God used to do in our lives, or to be mesmerized by a spiritual mountaintop experience of yesteryear is to miss the new and exciting victories God wants you to experience today.

We need to forget our *hurts* of the past. It is impossible to relate to others without being hurt from time to time. A slight, a snide remark, a misunderstanding of our motives or feelings—all of us have experienced such hurts. So had Paul! But he learned to turn these over to God.

We need to forget our *failures* of the past. Blunders mar our efforts every day of our lives. We deny Christ at times. We ignore him at others. Every person has those moments of denial when, like Simon Peter in the courtyard, we look up to see the hurt in Jesus' eyes and feel so guilty that we want to die. Think of Paul's past! But Paul had found forgiveness for his failures through Jesus Christ.

Analyze your conversation about spiritual matters. Is your conversation in the past tense or the present tense? Is God at work in your life now? If not, you are probably hung up on the accomplishments, hurts, and failures of your past.

The past of every person is marked by spiritual victories and spiritual defeats, personal friendships and personal feuds, healing relationships and hurtful ones. But the past is behind us. We cannot recall it nor relive it. We can only learn from it. Paul's ability to forget what was behind him was one of the secrets of his greatness.

3. *Continuation*

Think of all the cities Paul had conquered for Christ! Consider all the flourishing churches he had organized, all of the epistles he had written, all of the significant accomplishments he had already made! Now picture him in the Roman jail, near the end of his life, with all those accomplishments behind him, writing this letter to the Philippian Christians. What did Paul say? "I've done enough and now I am ready to retire." No! Instead he said, "I do not regard myself as having laid hold of it yet; but . . . reaching forward to what lies ahead, I press on toward the goal" (vv. 13-14, NASB). Paul was willing to continue moving toward new heights.

Paul was convinced that there were always more mountains to climb, more lives to help, more churches to build, more personal victories to win, more sermons to preach, more work to be done. "I do not regard myself as having laid hold of it yet." So Paul continued in his commitment to Christ. That was the secret of his life.

The reason for the ineffectiveness of many churches today is that Christians have given up too soon. Too many have retired, taken a sabbatical, and hung up their spiritual uniform, when they ought to be still running the race.

A friend of chewing gum magnate, Wrigley, was sitting by him on a plane. He asked Wrigley why he continued to advertise so extensively when his business was already so successful. The astute businessman responded, "For the same reason the pilot of this airplane keeps the engines running when we are already in the air."[22]

Paul refused to live on the momentum of yesterday's victories. He was too busy facing the challenge of tomorrow's opportunities.

When S. M. Lockridge received the Outstanding Alumni Award from Southwestern Baptist Theological Seminary in June, 1980, he said, "With this honor comes a new surge of desire for preaching. I am going to preach until Jesus calls or until he comes." So must we all, like Paul, "press on toward the goal for the prize of the upward call of God in Christ Jesus" (v. 14), until Jesus calls or until he comes.

COLOSSIANS

51. The Sufficiency of Christ

Colossians 1:15-18

A boy said to his girlfriend one night, "I don't have a lot of money like Jerome Green, but I sure do love you," to which she made no comment. Then the boy said, "I don't have a beautiful home like Jerome Green, but I really love you." Again, the girl was silent. "I don't have a brand-new Porsche like Jerome Green," added the boyfriend, "but you mean all the world to me." Finally, the girl responded, "I love you too, but tell me a little bit more abut Jerome Green."

How similarly we treat Christ in our statements to the world. We imply by our deeds and by our declarations that Jesus Christ is not much, that his offer cannot compare to the promises of the world. Then we wonder why people are more interested in learning about the world than they are about Christ. However, we do not have to apologize about this Christ who split history into BC and AD, for he is sufficient to meet every need in the life of man.

At no other place in the Bible do we find such a comprehensive picture of the sufficiency of Christ as Paul gave in his letter to the Christians at Colossae. In this Christological panorama, Paul presented a dramatic portrait of Christ.

1. *The Redeemer of Man* (vv. 13-14)

The dilemma of man is often underestimated today. We suggest that man is socially deprived, psychological maladjusted, or physically deficient. In contrast, the Bible declares that man is suffering from a sickness of the soul. Man is in the domain of darkness, under the power of evil, burdened by guilt from which he needs to be delivered. Christ is that Deliverer.

What does Jesus do to deliver man? First, he redeems us. He liberates us from the bondage of our sin through his sacrificial death on the cross. The writer of Hebrews expressed it like this: "Since then the children share in flesh and blood, He Himself likewise also partook of the same, that through death He might render powerless him who had the power of death, that is, the devil; and might deliver those who through fear of death were subject to slavery all their lives" (Heb. 2:14-15, NASB).

Then, he transfers us. As God removed the Israelites from their bondage in Egypt and transferred them into the Promised Land, even so Jesus removed the Christian from the land of darkness and transfers him into the land of light.

The need of man is met by Christ. He is man's Redeemer.

2. *The Revealer of God* (v. 15*a*)

Throughout the centuries, man has desired to know what God is like. Paul said that Christ came to give us that information, for Jesus is "the image of the invisible God." The word *image* (*eikon*) meant a direct impression, a precise reproduction. Jesus is a Xerox copy of God.

In Jesus we see not just another man, not just another teacher, not just another religious leader. Instead, we see God himself. Jesus revealed to us what God is like. This is the point of Jesus' dialogue with Philip at the Last Supper. Philip expressed the heartfelt desire of the centuries: "Lord, show us the Father, and it is enough for us." Jesus responded, "Have I been so long with you, and yet you have not come to know Me, Philip? He who has seen Me has seen the Father" (John 14:8,9, NASB).

Man's quest for God is met in Jesus. He is the Revealer of God.

3. *The Regent of the World* (vv. 15*b*-17)

Paul also described Jesus' relationship to the world. Paul proclaims him to be a cosmic Christ who preceded, produced, and preserves the world. "First-born" conveys the idea of priority of position, not previous birth. Before anything else existed, Jesus already existed. Jesus, who was prior to all things, is the One who produced all that is. He also preserves the world, for Paul said "in Him all things hold together."

A father wanted to keep his child busy one evening so he cut up a picture of the world and asked her to put it together. In just a few minutes she returned, with the world already together. In amazement the father asked how she had done it so quickly. "There was a picture of Jesus on the back," the little girl explained. "I put him together because I knew that if Jesus was in the right place, the world would be right!"

Jesus is the one who makes sense out of life. He is the regent of the world.

4. *The Ruler of the Church* (v. 18)

The "He" in verse 18 is emphatic. Not some preacher, not some philosopher, not some group of powerful laymen, not the feelings of the membership but he, himself, is the head of the church.

John Henry Jowett has rightly declared, "The multitude is not sick of Jesus; it is only sick of His feeble and bloodless representatives. When once again a great church appears, a church with the Lord's name in her forehead, a church with fine muscular limbs, and a face seamed with the marks of sacrifice, the multitude will turn their feet to the way of God's commandments."[23] A great church is one which allows Jesus Christ to be the head.

Let's not misunderstand the Baptist idea of autonomy. Some suggest that autonomy means a Baptist church can do anything it wants to do. No! Autonomy means that a church is free to do what Christ wants it to do. When a group of Christians do what they want to do, they may call themselves Baptists, but they are not the church. Jesus Christ is the head of the church. He sets the agenda. He rules.

Conclusion

Count Zinzendorf, the founder of the Moravians, was converted in an art gallery as he contemplated a painting of Christ on the cross. The picture was inscribed: "I did this for thee. What hast thou done for me?" The painting was done by a famous artist more than three hundred years earlier. The artist gave special attention to the face of Christ. After he had finished the first sketch of Jesus' face, he called in the landlady's little daughter. He asked her whom she thought it was. She replied, "It is a good man."

The painter realized that he had failed in his purpose, so he destroyed the painting and began again. After much prayer and work, he finished a second sketch of Christ's face. Again, he called in the girl and asked her whom it was. "He looks like a man who has really suffered," said the girl.

Once more the artist destroyed the sketch and after much prayer began a third. When this third portrait was finished, he asked the girl in again and asked her who it was. Looking at the face of Christ, the girl exclaimed, "It is the Lord."[24] As we lift up Christ, others will see him as the Lord. And they will find life in him.

1 THESSALONIANS

52. Thanks in All Things

1 Thessalonians 5:18

Several years ago a magazine publisher polled a number of prominent people all over the world to see what they desired most. Many interesting answers came in. One man, an architect, wished simply for a garden and a greenhouse. A noted writer wished for health. One public official said, "Give me a little Vermont farm with a brook and an apple orchard and I'll be satisfied." A gifted author wanted the ability to understand the language of animals. Perhaps the best answer was that of a man who said, "What I desire most of all is an ever greater ability to appreciate what I already have."[25]

This was a specialty for Paul. He had learned the secret of a thankful life. The basic characteristic of his life was expressed in our text: "In everything give thanks, for this is God's will for you in Christ Jesus." Paul did not just proclaim that principle. He practiced it as well. Paul was thankful in all things.

1. *The Savior*

Paul was thankful for Jesus Christ. Paul's exclamation in his letter to the Corinthians, "Thanks be unto God for his unspeakable gift" (2 Cor. 9:15, KJV), was repeated in one form or another in every letter he wrote. Paul's encounter with Christ on the Damasus road was the pivotal experience in his life. For the sake of Jesus, Paul was willing to sacrifice everything. "I count all things to be loss," he wrote to the Philippians, "in view of the surpassing value of knowing Christ Jesus as my Lord" (Phil. 3:8, NASB).

2. *Salvation*

Paul was thankful not only for who Jesus was but also for what Jesus had done. Jesus had transformed him and given him a new life. Jesus is the one who gave meaning to Paul's life.

Salvation to Paul meant to be saved *from* something. Paul knew the reality of guilt. He felt the judgment of God's law. He experienced the burden of his sinful nature. Christ saved him from all that.

Salvation also meant to be saved *for* something. Paul believed that God had set him apart to be his messenger to the Gentiles (Rom. 1:1-5), and to this purpose Paul committed his life.

Paul was thankful for salvation because he had been set free from his sin and set free for service.

3. *Strength*

Paul was thankful for the power Jesus provided in his daily life. "I thank Christ Jesus our Lord," Paul wrote to young Timothy, "who has strengthened me" (1 Tim. 1:12, NASB). To the Philippians he made a similar declaration: "I can do all things through Him who strengthens me" (Phil. 4:13, NASB). Paul was saved on the Damascus road. But as he walked up and down the roads which tied the Roman world together, he came to know the strengthening presence of the Lord. God not only saves; he also sustains. There is no problem you will ever face, no mountain you will ever have to climb, no task you will ever have to do, that God will not give you the strength to accomplish. As you step out in faith, you will discover as Paul did, "And my God shall supply all your needs according to His riches in glory in Christ Jesus" (Phil. 4:19, NASB).

4. *The Saints*

Paul was thankful for his fellow Christians. To the Romans, Paul wrote, "I thank my God through Jesus for you all" (Rom. 1:8, NASB). To the Corinthians he said, "I thank my God always concerning you" (1 Cor. 1:4, NASB). To the Ephesians he declared, . . . "I do not cease giving thanks for you" (Eph. 1:16, NASB). To the Philippians he exclaimed, "I thank my God in all my remembrance of you" (Phil. 1:3,

NASB). Paul had a profound sense of gratitude for his co-workers, for those fellow servants in every church who shared with him in the spread of the Gospel. He realized that he could never make it without them.

A retired preacher, looking back over his long career, said that he passed through three stages of understanding. During the first stage, the people of his congregation were in the river. He was on the bank telling them how to get out of the river and up to the bank where he was. In the next stage, he was on the edge of the bank, reaching down to help the people get up on the bank where he was. In the final stage, he realized that he was in the river with the people. They were holding him up, and underneath them all were the everlasting arms of God.[26]

When we think of those who have taught us and prayed us through crises, when we remember those who are sustaining us through prayer, we too must join with Paul in saying, "I thank my God through Jesus for you all" (Rom. 1:8, NASB).

5. *Suffering*

Paul was thankful for his difficulties. To the Colossian Christians Paul wrote, "Now I rejoice in my sufferings, for your sake" (Col. 1:24, NASB).

Do you know why Paul was thankful for his suffering? First, because in his suffering he reached the end of his own ability, and he was forced to really trust in God. This was the meaning of Paul's statement to the Corinthians: "But we have this treasure in earthen vessels, that the surpassing greatness of the power may be of God and not from ourselves" (2 Cor. 4:7, NASB).

Second, because his suffering enabled him to more ably minister to others who suffered. Paul opened his second letter to the Corinthians with a reference to a tragedy through which he had just passed. He explained the result of this experience of suffering by saying that God "comforts us in all our affliction so that we may be able to comfort those who are in any affliction with the comfort with which we ourselves are comforted by God" (2 Cor. 1:4, NASB).

Third, because he knew that his suffering could not compare with the glory that God was preparing for him (Rom. 8:18). Some young person suggested that the pay for following Christ is not that good, but his retirement plan is out of sight! Suffering is not the final word in the life of the Christian.

"In everything give thanks, for this is God's will for you in Christ Jesus."

2 THESSALONIANS

53. These Things We Believe

2 Thessalonians 2:15

One of the young people of our church was deeply troubled as she came to see me. She had been involved in a religious discussion at school. A Roman Catholic youth and a member of the Mormon tradition were discussing their respective beliefs. Both ably articulated the basic doctrines of their faith. When the young lady who was a member of my church was brought into the discussion, her ignorance became very evident. She became painfully aware that she did not understand what our denomination believed.

Evangelicals have a rich heritage. Our members need to be informed about it. And they need to be continuously instructed on our distinctives which are a part of that heritage. In order to "stand firm and hold to the traditions" as Paul suggested in our text, our people have to be taught these distinctives.

So what do evanglicals believe? I'm a Baptist, and we have many basic beliefs in common with other Christians.

1. *The Primacy of the Scripture*

In early America, for instance, Baptists were avoided because one could not meet a Baptist without the Baptist trying to cram the Bible down his throat. Although we disapprove of the methods of these early Baptists, we do share their heritage, for we are people of the Book.

All great doctrines of our faith, all other distinctives, find their sources in the Scriptures. The Bible alone is our creed.

We believe that the Bible is the Word of God. Second Peter 1:21 (NASB) declares that "No prophecy was ever made by an act of the human will, but men moved by the Holy Spirit spoke from God." The Bible is not man's words about God. It is God's Word to man.

We believe that the Word of God will last forever. The Bible has been scrutinized, analyzed, and dichotomized throughout the centuries. Many skeptics have sought to destroy the Bible, but it has been an anvil that has worn out many hammers. First Peter 1:14 (NASB) affirms that, "ALL FLESH IS LIKE GRASS, AND ALL ITS GLORY LIKE THE FLOWER OF GRASS, THE GRASS WITHERS, AND THE FLOWER FALLS OFF, BUT THE WORD OF THE LORD ABIDES FOREVER."

We believe that the Word of God has the power to change lives. When God's Word is studied and applied to our lives, we will never be the same. The Scriptures are primary in the life of the believer.

2. *The Plan of Salvation*

The basic question of life is, how can a person be right with God? We believe that there is only one answer to that question: salvation.

Salvation comes through God's grace. Grace is "God's riches at Christ's expense." Salvation is a gift from God through his Son Jesus Christ (Eph. 2:8-9).

Any person can appropriate this gift of salvation through faith (Rom. 10:13). Faith's acrostic means "Forsaking all I trust him."

This salvation, by grace through faith, lasts forever. All true believers endure to the end. Those who put their trust in Christ will never fall away. They may fall into sin through neglect. They may grieve the Spirit of God by their unconcern. They may impair their spiritual growth by indifference. But nothing can ever separate a Christian from the love of God in Christ Jesus (Rom. 8:38-39).

3. *The Priesthood of the Saints*

A priest had two functions in the Bible. He brought the needs of the people to God. He was also the agent through whom the grace of God was delivered to man. The key word is access. The priest had access to God and was the mediator for man. Jesus Christ made us all priests before God! Jesus broke down the wall which separated man and God and made it possible for all of us to have access to God (Rom. 5:1-2).

4. *The Participation of the Saved*

Every Christian should belong to a local church so he can participate in the ongoing of God's work. Paul told the Ephesian Christians that we are "created in Christ Jesus for good works" (Eph. 2:10).

Beginning in Genesis and weaving its way through the Bible is the incredible truth that God has chosen us to be the agents by which his world is administered and his work is accomplished. We are to be his stewards (1 Cor. 4:1), his ambassadors (2 Cor. 5:20), his workmanship (Eph. 2:10), his witnesses (Acts 1:8). Therefore, every Christian should be involved in a local church where we can carry out the purpose for which we have been redeemed.

5. *The Principle of Separation*

Our denomination has stood firmly for the conviction of the separation of church and state from the beginning. This does not suggest noninvolvement in politics by a Christian. Rather, it is the declaration that no government, no state, and no political leader has the right to tell an individual Christian how to believe or what to believe. As Bill Self put it, "What God hath rent asunder, let no man join together."

6. *The Priority of Sharing*

From our inception, we have been evangelistic people who have taken the commission of Jesus to his disciples (Matt. 28:19-20) to be our marching orders.

Once a shoe salesman was sent to Africa. He cabled the company in two weeks saying, "Send money to come home. No one wears shoes here." Another salesman was sent. Two weeks later he sent a telegram which said, "Send all the shoes you have. I have never seen so many prospects."

That is the way we look at the world. We see people hungry

for the message of God, and we believe in sharing God's Word to them.

This missionary spirit begins at home. The missionary vision continues to expand until all the world is encompassed. Mission involvement and concern have always been the heartbeat of our life.

7. *The Preeminence of the Savior*

Our motto through the years has been Ephesians 1:22: "And so He has put all things under His feet and made Him (Jesus Christ) the supreme Head of the church" (Williams). Because of who Jesus is and because of what Jesus has done, we believe that he is to have preeminence in everything we do.

These things we believe. Let us "stand firm and hold to the traditions" which we have been taught.

1 TIMOTHY

54. Committed to What?

1 Timothy 4:1-11

Paul's predictions in his first epistle to young Timothy are being fulfilled in our day. All around us are examples of the false teachings cited in our text. Those who give attention to deceitful doctrines (v. 1) are proliferating in America as the New Consciousness groups increase in number.

Those who focus on demonology (v. 1) are becoming more common on the American religious scene. There are more than one hundred thousand practicing witches in America today. Nearly seventy institutions of higher learning in our country offer courses in witchcraft. Those who ascribe to a false asceticism (v. 3) are also apparent in our day. Two wanderers dressed in white robes who recently came by our church told me that they were traveling over all the earth, keeping themselves pure for Christ. No meat, no impure food, no sex—that was their standard of living.

In the midst of the confusion created by this spread of false teachings, we must not forget that Christ calls us to a life of commitment. Commitment is to be the mark of our lives. But committed to what? That is the question Paul answered in our text.

1. *To a Person*

First, we are to be committed to a person, Jesus Christ. Paul warned Timothy of a time of falling away from the faith and of discouragement for the church. When that happens, this is what Paul suggested in verse 6, "Be a good servant of Jesus Christ." Our commitment must go first, not to a certain church or to a certain program or to a certain style of music or to a certain preacher, but our commitment is first of all to Christ. He is to be Lord over our lives.

Jack Taylor's book, *The Key to Triumphant Living*, has been a phenomenal success. The basic message of the book is that a person must die to self and let Christ be Lord of all and in all. That is not a new message. Faithful preachers of the Word have been proclaiming that message to the world in every generation. That is the clarion call which has emanated from the church since the first century. To be a Christian is to die to our desires, our wills, our feelings, our ambitions, and let Christ be not just our friend, not just our companion, not just our teacher, not just our Savior, but our Lord.

When we become a Christian, we are no longer our own. We belong body and soul to Jesus Christ. We are committed to a person.

2. *To a Pattern*

This commitment to the person of Christ will lead then to a commitment to a new pattern of living. Paul urged Timothy in verse 7: "Discipline yourself for the purpose of godliness." A Christian is committed not only to Christ but also to the pattern of living Christ laid out for us. That pattern is one of holiness, purity, and godliness.

The world in which we live is one committed to pleasure and self. Consequently, the life-style of the world is that of immorality and selfishness. That pattern of living is in stark contrast to the life-style commanded by Jesus. On one hand is the world's way. On the other is the way of Jesus Christ. A Christian is committed to the way of Jesus Christ.

Dr. J. Wilbur Chapman once gave this rule of thumb for determining our pattern of living. He said: "Anything that dims my vision of Christ, or takes away my taste for Bible study, or cramps my prayer life, or makes Christian work more difficult is wrong for me, and I must, as a Christian, turn away from it."[27]

So must every true Christian. We cannot call ourselves by

Christ's name and still be free to do our own thing. When we call ourselves by his name, we are committing ourselves to do his thing.

3. *To a People*

We are also to be committed to a people, to the church of Jesus Christ. In verse 6, Paul told Timothy that a good servant to Christ was one who is "constantly nourished on the words of the faith and of the sound doctrine." In verse 13 he added, "Until I come, give attention to the public reading of Scripture, to exhortation and teaching." Translated into today's terms, Paul said that a Christian is one who spends time with other believers in the study of God's Word in the church.

D. T. Niles told of a member of his congregation whom he met on the street one day. She had been active once but in recent months drifted away. She was suffering numerous personal and family problems. It was a time of stress in her life. She told Niles that God had become distant to her, that she had lost her contact with him, and that religion did not seem to mean much to her anymore.

This was how Niles answered her: "Not only now but even in the future, there will always be times when God seems distant; when it looks as if God has forgotten and does not care; when prayers go unanswered and life is difficult. And at such times you must learn to hold onto your fellow Christians. Your difficulty is that you tried to hold on to God alone, and man was never intended to hold on to God alone."[28]

Man was never intended to hold onto God alone! What a great truth for us to be captured by. The church is to be the believer's life-support system, from which strength comes for the living of these days.

4. *To a Program*

A Christian is also to be committed to a program. This program is described in verse 11: "Prescribe and teach these things." The program to which every Christian should be committed is the program called witnessing. In a world when so many are fanatics about the wrong thing, we must share with the world the one who said, "I am the way, and the truth, and the life; no one comes to the Father, but through Me" (John 14:6, NASB).

A young single woman came to Christ and made her decision public. As she shared her decision with the pastor, she said, "Please pray for me. I am working in an office with twenty other girls, and not one of them is a Christian." Six weeks later, she brought a friend to her pastor. "This is the sixteenth one I have reached," she explained. "The other four are scared to death, because they know that their turn will be next!"

That is a portrait of a Christian. Commit yourself to a person, Jesus Christ. Then, commit yourself to the pattern of living he has laid out for you. Next, commit yourself to the people he has left in this world to extend his kingdom. Finally, you commit yourself to the program he himself established for the spreading of his good news. Such commitment will bring clarity in a day of confusion.

2 TIMOTHY

55. The Book of Books

2 Timothy 3:14-16

On November 19, 1863, Abraham Lincoln went to a town called Gettysburg to speak at the dedication of a national cemetery. His immortal words spoken on that occasion have persevered throughout the ages since then. They were not, however, so highly thought of at the time of their delivery. A newspapter editor in Harrisburg who heard Lincoln's address, wrote this review in the paper the next day: "We pass over the silly remarks of the President; for the credit of the nation, we are willing that the veil of oblivion shall be dropped over them and that they shall no more be repeated or thought of."[29]

Many have reflected that same skepticism toward the words of the Bible. They consider the words of the Scriptures to be silly, senseless, and irrelevant to today's living. In contrast, for the people of faith, there is no book that has ever been written whose words are so profound, whose truths are so timeless, whose heroes are so inspiring, whose message is so uplifting, as is the Book, the Bible.

Belief in the Bible is at the heart of our faith. But what do we believe about the Bible?

1. *An Inspired Book*

We believe that the Bible is an inspired book. "All Scripture," Paul wrote, "is inspired by God." The word translated *inspired* (v. 16) is the Greek word which means *God-breathed*." The Bible is a book that comes from the very mouth of God, breathed out by him.

This truth is proclaimed on almost every page of the Old Testament. Expressions such as "God said" or "The Lord spoke" occur in the Pentateuch 680 times, in the historical books 418 times, and in the prophetic writings 1,307 times. As Peter put it in his epistle, "For the prophecy came not in old times by the will of man: but holy men of God spake as they were moved by the Holy Ghost" (2 Pet. 1:21).

These statements, of course, refer to the Old Testament. In Galatians 1:11-12 and 1 Corinthians 2:10-12, Paul applied the same idea of inspiration to the message of the first apostles which became the New Testament. Their message, too, came from God. It was God-breathed.

Men of every age have affirmed that the Bible is a God-breathed, inspired book. But what does that mean? It means that the Bible is not just another book written by man but a Book whose author is God. The Bible is not just the book of the month but the Book of all eternity. The Bible is not the words of man. It is the Word of God. It is an inspired Book.

2. *An Informative Book*

The Bible is also an informative book. Everything we need to know about God, everything we need to know about what God has done, everything we need to know about what God wants us to do, is found in his Holy Word.

We spend a lot of time reading the newspapers. That's all right, for we do need to understand what is going on in our world. We spend much time reading magazines. That's all right, because we need to know what people are doing. We spend many hours reading novels. That's all right, too, for we need to know where people are coming from in our world. Even more important, however, is to spend our time reading the Bible for it is here that we understand what God is doing in our world and where he is coming from, and where we are going.

Paul said that the Bible is "profitable for teaching, for reproof, for correction, for training in righteousness" (v. 16). It is to the Bible we must go to discover how to live out our Christian lives. The Bible is the information book for the Christian life.

3. *An Inexhaustive Book*

The Bible is also an inexhaustive book. Statistics tell us that of every 1,000 books written, 650 are forgotten at the end of a year. One hundred and fifty more are forgotten by the end of three years. Only fifty survive as long as seven years. Why? Because times change, expressions vary, and needs fluctuate. Yet the Bible is a book completed almost 1,900 years ago, and it continues to be a best-seller in our day.

There is a uniqueness about the Bible that makes it inexhaustive. Augustine once said, "The Holy Spirit has with admirable wisdom and care for our welfare, so arranged the Holy Scriptures as by the plainer passages to satisfy our hunger, and by the more obscure to stimulate our appetite."[30]

The more we know about the Bible, the more we want to know. The more we study the Bible, the more we discover we do not know. It is an inexhaustible Book.

4. *An Inspirational Book*

The Bible is also an inspirational Book. Notice the way Paul put it in verse 17. The result of the study of God's Word is that "the man of God may be adequate, equipped for every good work." The word translated *adequate* is a word which means to be made complete or whole. Study of the Word of God makes us a whole person, adequate for every need, equipped for every responsibility.

Several years ago I read an article entitled, "How the Bible Can Help Us Solve Today's Problems." The article was the response of four prominent clergymen to the question, "What is the most serious problem facing the nation today, and which Bible passages can help solve them?"

Dr. Norman Vincent Peale, Pastor of the Marble Collegiate Church in New York, said that the greatest problem of our day is the deterioration of character which stems from moral laxity. The answer is God's prescription in 2 Chronicles 7:14. For the moral laxity of our day, the Bible offers One in whose strength and according to whose guidance we can once more live a moral life.

Dr. W. A. Criswell, pastor of the First Baptist Church in Dallas, Texas, said that the greatest problem confronting America was the lack of a firm foundation upon which to build our lives. The answer to the problem is found in 1 Corinthians 3:11. For the instability of our day, the Bible offers One upon whom a firm life can be built.

Cardinal Cody, the Roman Catholic Archbishop of Chicago, said the greatest problem in America today is what to do with the challenges of the modern world. The answer to the problem Cardinal Cody found in a phrase repeated several times in the New Testament: "Fear Not!" To modern man, on the brink of new frontiers, the Bible gives a message of courage.

Julius Mark, rabbi emeritus of the Temple Emanuel in New York, said that the greatest problem of modern man is a lack of hope in the future. The answer he found in the coming Messiah. We Christians find our hope in the fact that this Messiah who has already come will come again, "that at the name of Jesus every knee should bow . . . and . . . every tongue should confess that Jesus Christ is Lord, to the glory of God the Father" (Phil. 2:9-10, NASB).

For the needs facing modern man—the deterioration of morality, the lack of a firm foundation, fear before the challenges of our time, a lack of hope in the future—the answer is to be found in the Bible. The Bible is not only inspired; it is inspiring. It is not only from God; it is for man. It not only speaks the truth; its truth will set you free. It is indeed the Book of books!

TITUS

56. What It Means to Be a Servant

Titus 1:1

Walking along the street one day, a lady noticed a little boy trying to ring a doorbell that he could not quite reach. She went over and picked him up so that he could reach the bell. He rang it several times. "What now?" asked the lady. The little boy answered, "Run like crazy!"

There are many people who, after having become Christians, wonder "What now? Now that I have been redeemed from the bondage of Satan and released from the burden of my sin, what should I do?" In the introduction of his epistle to Titus, Paul gave an answer to that question in the appellative that he applied to himself. He called himself a servant of Jesus Christ.

There are several Greek words used for servant. A *diakonos* was a servant who ministered. A *therapon* was an attendant. An *oiketes* was a domestic, a house servant. A *misthios* was a hired servant. None of these are the words Paul used in the text. He used the word *doulos* which literally means slave. It refers to one who is in a relationship to another which only death can break. Paul said that the most descriptive word to explain his relationship to the Lord was the word *slave.* He was a bond servant, a slave of Jesus Christ. If we are to understand what we are to do now that we have become Christians, we need to come to a clearer understanding of what it means to be a servant.

1. *Identified with Christ*

A servant was identified with his master. This is seen in both the meaning of the word, *doulos,* and in the common practice of the day. *Doulos* is derived from a word that means "to bind." That is, a slave was one who was bound or connected to another. Slaves were commonly marked with visible signs, similar to brands, which identified them with their master. A slave, then, was one whose whole identity was derived from the one to whom he belonged.

Paul had this idea of identity in mind when he called himself a servant of Jesus Christ. He was no longer his own. He had been bought with the price of the blood of Jesus Christ, and now he belonged to him (1 Cor. 6:20). Paul's whole life pointed to Christ; his total identity was found in Christ. He was identified with him.

Now examine yourself. When someone watches your life and hears your speech and examines your relationships and sees your reactions, can he tell that you belong to the Lord? Does your life identify you with the life of the Master? That's what it means to be a servant.

2. *Obedient to Christ*

A slave was not only identified with his master. He was also obedient to his master.

A Roman centurion came to Jesus one day. He was a man with authority over his forces. He told Jesus, "I have the authority over my soldiers. I can say to the man go, and he will go; and to another come and he will come; and to my servant do this and he will do it" (Matt. 8:9, author's translation). A servant's one concern is to discern his master's will so he can obey it. So it is in our relationship to Christ. Christ is our Master. That means he has authority over our lives. To call ourselves his slave means that we are obedient to him.

What is it that determines right and wrong for us? For the Christian there is but one answer. Jesus determines right and wrong for us, and he reveals it to us through his written Word and by his indwelling Spirit. If he says to do it, it's right. If he says not to, it's wrong—because we are his servants, and we are to be obedient to him. That's what it means to be a servant.

3. *Ministering for Christ*

The idea of servanthood included the additional dimension of ministry. Paul combined the ideas of stewardship and servanthood in 1 Cor. 4:1 (NASB): "Let a man regard us in this manner, as servants of Christ, and stewards of the mysteries of God. In this case, morever, it is required of stewards that one be found trustworthy." In 1 Peter 4:10, Christians are called "stewards of the manifold grace of God." The Bible says that Jesus Christ is the Lord of the cosmos. In other words, he is the general manager of the universe. But he has appointed every Christian to be his assistant manager. As his servants, our responsibility is to care for his world and carry out his work.

We are to do what man was originally commissioned to do but failed to do because of his sin. We are to "fill the earth and subdue it; and have dominion over" it (Gen. 1:28, RSV). We are to be stewards of the mysteries of God. We are to minister for him. That's what it means to be a servant.

4. *Supplied by Christ*

For all the bad aspects of the institution of slavery there was one distinct benefit. The slave had no worry about his supplies. His clothes, his food, his medical treatment, his housing, everything was provided by his master.

When Paul called himself a slave of Jesus Christ, it brought a sense of contentment in his heart for he knew that now he could rely on Christ for all his resources. He expressed this idea clearly in the closing verses of the letter to the Philippians when he said, "My God shall supply all your needs according to his riches in glory in Christ Jesus" (Phil. 4:19, NASB).

When we rely on friends, we get what cooperation can provide. When we rely on our own skill, we get what human ability can provide. When we rely on our finances, we have what money can provide. But when we rely on Christ, we get what God can provide! A servant is one who relies on God and knows that God's work in God's way will never lack supplies.

5. *Conclusion*

Everybody is a slave to something. The idea of complete freedom is a myth. Whatever is most important in your life is your master. Being a slave of Jesus Christ will give you the greatest freedom to realize the potential God planted within you. It will not cramp your style. It will release you. When you make yourself his servant, you are putting yourself under the control of the one who made you, knows you, and loves you. You'll have freedom from the fickleness of your feelings, freedom from the contradictions of your conscience, freedom from the pressure of your peers, freedom from the wooing of the world, freedom from the motivation of the moment, freedom to be what God made you to be. Freedom to be you! That is the result of being a servant of Jesus Christ.

PHILEMON

57. The Church in Your House

Philemon 2

Say the word *church* and it brings to our mind a beautiful building where Christians gather to worship, a building with stained-glass windows, high arched ceilings, a magnificent organ, and a spire jutting toward the heavens. Church is a place we go to on Sunday morning. Paul gave the word *church* a new twist when he spoke of "the church in your house" (v. 2).

What did Paul mean? He was writing to Philemon. Did he mean simply that the local church met in Philemon's house each time they came together in worship? Perhaps.

But let me suggest another possible meaning of that key phrase, "the church in your house." Maybe Paul was describing the character of Philemon's home. Perhaps Paul meant, "the atmosphere of your home and your actions in it make your home seem like a church."

Although some churches do meet in people's homes today, we are not likely to ever do that again on a full scale. However, no greater need faces modern America than to live in our homes in such a way that they are like a church.

What will it take to have the church in your house?

1. *Walk with the Lord*

One pastor described the home as "a hothouse where in a certain isolation of sheltered loyalties beautiful things are grown—affections, sympathies, insights, devotions—which afterwards can be transplanted and applied to the common good of humankind."[31]

What kind of atmosphere exists in your home? Is encouragement the basic characteristic or is criticism? Is expectancy the dominant mood, or is despair? Is faith the foundation of your family, or is self? Is worship descriptive of the atmosphere of your home, or is worldliness?

Your walk will determine your children's walk. The oft-repeated poem is nevertheless true: Children learn what they live.

"If a child lives with criticism, he learns to condemn.
"If a child lives with hostility, he learns to fight.
"If a child lives with fear, he learns to be apprehensive.
"If a child lives with pity, he learns to be sorry for himself.
"If a child lives with jealousy, he learns to feel guilty.
"If a child lives with encouragement, he learns to be confident.
"If a child lives with tolerance, he learns to be patient.
"If a child lives with acceptance, he learns to love.
"If a child lives with approval, he learns to like himself.
"If a child lives with recognition, he learns to have a goal.
"If a child lives with fairness, he learns to have faith in himself.
"If a child lives with honesty, he learns what truth is.
"If a child lives with friendliness, he learns that the world is a nice place to live."

One little boy was asked why he believed in God? "Well," he replied, "I guess it just runs in the family." That was "the church in your house."

Sam Shoemaker, the famous Episcopal preacher, was asked how he came to believe in God. He explained, "Daddy didn't have to tell me about God. He believed in Him, and I caught it."[32] That was "the church in your house."

To have a church in your house means to walk with the Lord at home.

2. *Worship the Lord*

To have the church in your house, you must also worship at home. A spiritual atmosphere in your home is a result of spiritual actions. Prayer at mealtime and bedtime can be special times of communion with God. The reading of God's Word with the family is not some anachronistic relic of the past but a requirement for spiritual power in the present. A commitment to prayer and Bible study with the family can transform the home from a hotel where a family meets for food and rest into a sanctuary where a family meets God.

As the pastor visited in her home, one mother was very much concerned about making the proper impression. She called to her daughter, "Honey, bring the book that mother loves so much and reads so often." The little girl entered the room with the Sears catalogue!

To have the church in your house means to give priority attention to the Word of God, to communicating that Word to our children, and to leading them into an encounter with God.

3. *Witness for the Lord*

David Mace says that the home is the most powerful evangelizing force in the world. Some parents are afraid they will force their faith on their children. Much more tragic are those parents who refuse to give their children any faith at all.

In Jesus' command to his disciples, he said that our witness was to begin in Jerusalem (Acts 1:8). That means at home, with those closest to us. We are to share our faith with our children so they can have a framework in which to develop their own faith.

Cecil Osborne gives a beautiful illustration of this process. Suppose you inherit a large furnished house where your deceased parents lived. This is to be your new home. As you go through the house you see a wild assortment of furniture of all sorts and shapes. Simply shifting the furniture around does not help. So you take all of it out into the yard. Then you begin to experiment. One piece will go in a bedroom, another in the dining room, and so on. With the furniture you like, your home is now about half-furnished. Then, you buy the additional pieces you want. Finally, the house is yours. Although some of the furniture was your parents, it is no longer theirs. It is yours now.[33]

This is the way faith is shaped in the life of the child. The fundamentals are established, the seeds planted, but the necessary readjustment has to be made by the child. To have the church in your house means to give the child an inheritance out of which he can shape his faith.

4. *Conclusion*

A father was at the bedside of a son who was near death. The father, who was a Christian, was nevertheless heartbroken at the loss of his precious child. Seeing his father's tears, the boy said, "Don't cry, Dad. When I die, I'm going to heaven. And when I get to heaven, I'll walk right up to Jesus and tell him that it is because of you that I am there." That is the ultimate result of having "the church in your house."

HEBREWS

58. Faith

Hebrews 11:1—12:1

What is faith? In *The Devil's Dictionary*, a cynical look at Christianity, faith is defined as "belief without evidence in what is told by one who speaks without knowledge of things without parallel."[34] That's not far from the definition given by a youngster in Sunday School. "Faith," the child said, "is believing something you know isn't true."

What is faith? The clearest biblical answer is found in the eleventh chapter of Hebrews, for this is the faith chapter of the Bible. Twenty-three times the word *faith* appears in this chapter. The writer of Hebrews was not talking about faith in general but about a particular kind of faith. This faith, exemplified by the saints of God and illustrated in the life of Jesus, is a faith which puts us in touch with eternity. In this chapter we see:

1. *The Definition of Faith*

What is faith? The writer of Hebrews declared that faith means to believe that God is, "and that He is a rewarder of those who seek Him" (v. 6). J. B. Phillips catches the spirit of the verse in his translation. Faith means to believe "first that God exists and secondly, that it is worth a man's while to try to find God."

Faith is a special way of seeing. Faith is the insight that behind the visible world stands the invisible world. Behind the activities and movements of men are the activities and movements of God. Realizing that we live in two different worlds, faith perceives that the real world, the world that really counts, is the spiritual world.

In this chapter we also see:

2. *The Demonstration of Faith*

The writer of Hebrews not only described what faith is. He also declared what faith does.

Faith *chooses* (v. 25). Using the example of Moses, the writer of Hebrews declared that faith not only discerns two different worlds, the material and the spiritual, but it also definitely and deliberately chooses the spiritual. Faith opts for God.

Ittai was a faithful member of King David's army. During the difficult times of Absalom's rebellion, many of David's men were deserting him. David suggested that Ittai do the same. This was the response Ittai gave. "As the Lord liveth, and as my lord the king liveth, surely in what place my Lord the king shall be, whether in death or life, even there also will thy servant be" (2 Sam. 15:21).

That is a declaration of faith. Whether in life or death, whether in good times or in bad, faith deliberately and definitely decides for God.

Faith also *acts*. Notice the active words in this chapter. Abel offered (v. 4). Enoch walked (v. 5). Noah prepared (v. 7). Abraham went (v. 8). Faith not only chooses God. It goes to work for him. Faith is active.

An old New England statute said that when two vehicles approach an intersection, both are to stop until one proceeds! That's what happens in life. Everyone stops until someone proceeds. Consequently, we are insnared in the inane inadequacy of inactivity.

Faith, however, replaces inactivity with action. Faith sees a job, and does it. Faith sees a hurt heart, and reaches out a helping hand. Faith confronts a need, and meets it. Faith answers the challenge of God, "Whom shall I send?" with the response, "Send me." Faith acts.

Faith also *endures*. Beginning in verse 33, like a fast moving motion picture, the many attacks on faith are flashed before our eyes. But faith endures them all, and remains firm to the end.

Someone has suggested that "a faith that fizzles at the finish was faulty from the first." This is the message of our text. Real faith endures because it has its eyes on the invisible world; it has its ear attuned to God. Faith perceives that in the end, God will have the final word. Finally, the darkness of Friday will be eclipsed by the light of resurrection Sunday. So faith hangs on.

The writer of Hebrews gives us yet another insight on faith. Implied in verses 32–34 and clearly expressed in verse one of chapter twelve is:

3. *The Defense of Faith*

Following this discussion of faith is the statement: "We have a great cloud of witnesses surrounding us" (12:1). Two Greek words can be translated "cloud." The word *nephele* means a small detached, sharply outlined cloud. The word *nephos* means a mass of cloud.[35] It is the latter word which the writer of Hebrews used. The ones who have believed, the ones who have followed this faith approach to life, are so numerous that you cannot see the end of them. They are like a great mass of clouds which covers the whole sky.

That is a word we need to hear today. So often, like Elijah, we crawl back into our caves of discouragement and cry, "Lord, I am the only one who is really following you. I am the only one who is keeping the faith." The writer of Hebrews responded, "No, that is not so. You are not alone when you choose to align your life with God." Whenever this mood of discouragement grabs you, you need to remember again the picture painted in this chapter of the mighty host with whom we hold fellowship every time we come together in God's name. It is a great multitude which no man can number.

Consider the cloud of witnesses surrounding us.

See Peter and John standing before the Sanhedrin saying, "Whether it is right in the sight of God to give heed to you rather than to God, you be the judge; for we cannot stop speaking what we have seen and heard" (Acts 4:19).

Hear the Apostle Paul, on board a boat which seemed

doomed for destruction, in the midst of sailors bowed with despair, saying with confidence, "For this very night an angel of God to whom I belong and whom I serve stood before me, saying, 'Do not be afraid, Paul; you must stand before Caesar; and behold, God has granted you all those who are sailing with you.' Therefore keep up your courage, men, for I believe God, that it will turn out exactly as I have been told" (Acts 27:23-25, NASB).

See Polycarp in the coliseum of Rome with the voice of the emperor ringing out, "Polycarp, renounce your Christ, or you shall die," and hear him respond, "Caesar, accept my Christ, and you shall live."

Hear Joan of Arc, in the midst of the flames that consumed her physical body, crying out, "Jesus, Jesus, Jesus!"

See Martin Luther at the Council of Worms, standing before the most powerful force of his day, refusing to deny his faith with bold declaration, "Here I stand."

See John Bunyan in a loathsome prison declaring, "I am determined, God being my helper and shield, to stay here until the moss grows over my eyebrows rather than surrender my faith."

Don't you ever think you are alone when you are on God's side. When you back God against the world, walking by faith and not by sight, you are joining the procession of saints of every age who have believed that God is, and that it is worthwhile to serve him. If you are a part of that triumphant family of faith, you need to rejoice! If you are not, you need to repent, and put your life in God's hands. Faith is the victory that will eventually overcome the world.

JAMES

59. When Money Hurts

James 5:1-6

The man suffered from severe lower back pain which finally reached such intensity that he had to go to the doctor. His condition was initially diagnosed as a probable herniated spinal disk. Upon further investigation the doctor concluded that the man had a severe case of "wallet sciatica." The man requested an explanation in laymen's terms. The doctor asked him to take out his billfold. He pulled out a big, fat billfold full of credit cards. The doctor told him that the wallet was putting extreme pressure on the sciatic nerve and causing the symptoms. The prescription which led to an immediate cure was a "wallectomy;" that is, the removal of the offending wallet.

The Bible has a great deal to say about money and its effect on man. The Bible does not say that money is evil. Neither does the Bible declare that having an excess of money is a sin. It was this misunderstanding that led Emperor Julian of the Roman Empire to once state that he would confiscate all of the Christian wealth so that they could be poor and thus enter into the kingdom of heaven!

The Bible's position is that money is neutral. It can be used to bring glory to God and thus be an incomparable blessing. Or, as James put it in verse one of the text, money can cause men to weep and howl. Money can help or hurt.

When does money hurt?

1. *When We Use It Wrongly*

The basic theme of the Bible is not that it is wrong to have money, but that it is wrong for your money to have you. Money becomes a danger when, instead of using it to further the kingdom of God, we use it to foster an indulgent, extravagant life-style for ourselves. James condemned his contemporaries because they "have lived in high style on the earth." Money is bad when it is used wrongly. That's the counsel of God's Word.

This message of the Bible, however, has been silenced by the modern world's lunge toward luxury. Our insatiable desire for more has spawned credit buying and financial overextension which has many people on the brink of disaster. The problem is that our yearning capacity has exceeded our earning capacity.

One wealthy man, when asked the secret of his financial success, said it was his wife. Then he explained: "I wanted to see if there was any income she could not live beyond."

Another man refused to report to the police about his wife's credit cards being stolen. He figured the thief would use them less than she did!

When we use our money wrongly it hurts us, not only financially but spiritually. Instead of controlling our money, we find ourselves in a situation where our money controls us. And we miss out on the investments in spiritual things which will reap eternal dividends. Money can hurt when we use it wrongly.

2. *When We Get It Wrongly*

Many have felt that as long as you use your money wisely and for a good cause, it doesn't matter how you get it. Not so. The Bible speaks as strongly against those who get their money in the wrong way as it does against those who use it in the wrong way.

This was the message of the prophets. Amos condemned those who trample the needy, who make the bushel smaller and the shekel bigger and cheat with dishonest scales (Amos 8:5). Malachi spoke against those who oppressed the hireling in his wages (Mal. 3:5). Isaiah prophesied against those aristocratic land-grabbers who joined house to house until the rural area was turned into a series of great estates reducing the farmers to the status of slaves (Isa. 5:8). The prophets denounced those who earned their money wrongly.

This was the message of Jesus. His was an ethics of love. Treat others in the way you wanted them to treat you. That was the counsel of the Master. Jesus recommended a love which went beyond our actions to our attitudes, which would not dare oppress anyone else because they were our brothers. Jesus would not tolerate those who earned their money wrongly.

This, too, was the message of James in our text. Evidently there were Christians who would hire workers to cut their fields, but then would not pay them when they were through. James said that the outcry of those who did the harvesting had reached the ears of God.

The message is the same throughout the Bible. Money hurts when injustice and inhumanity, dishonesty and deception are the methods by which it is obtained.

3. *When We Value It Wrongly*

This is the bottom line of the whole money issue. Why do we use loveless methods to obtain money? Why will we use our money to settle down in the lap of luxury? Because we value money wrongly. Because we make money our god. How often life is measured on the basis of its monetary value.

A small-town, weekly newspaper described the robbery and murder of a local businessman. He was waylaid after work on Saturday night on his way home. The newspaper article stated, "Fortunately for the deceased, he had just deposited his day's receipts in the bank, with the result that he lost nothing but his life!" Wasn't he fortunate?

Money hurts when we exalt it as the most important thing in life, our chief goal for which we strive, and the panacea for all of our ills. James reminded us in our text that money is neither permanent nor lasting. It can rot away like grain. It can be destroyed like moth-eaten cloth. It can rust like metal. Therefore, money is not to be attributed ultimate value.

Material possessions are not our most valuable possessions,

for there are some things money will not do. One man was most certainly right when he said that money is "a universal passport to everything except heaven and a universal provider of everything except happiness."

You may not have wallet sciatica. But your money can still hurt you—if you use it wrongly, if you get it wrongly, or if you value it wrongly.

1 PETER

60. Making God Look Good

1 Peter 2:12-18

Paul told the Corinthian Christians that we are to glorify God in all things (1 Cor. 10:31). In our text, Peter declared that we are to so live that others might see our good deeds and glorify God (1 Pet. 2:12). To glorify God is to be the chief end of man, the primary purpose of the Christian.

What does the word *glorify* mean? The Greek word translated *to glorify* appears in the New Testament fifty-eight times. A close study of those passages will reveal the following meanings conveyed by the words: *to magnify, to honor, to laud,* and *to exalt.* Webster's definition is more precise. To glorify means "to make, or make seem, better, larger, or more beautiful."[36] To glorify God, then, means to make God look good to those who are around us, to make him seem better, larger, and more beautiful.

How are we to accomplish that feat? Peter offered several suggestions in our text.

1. *Be a Good Neighbor*

We glorify God when we "honor all men" (v. 17). The word translated *honor* conveys the idea of respect or dignity. Honor is an attitude adopted toward an exalted personage. Peter said that we are to adopt that attitude toward all men.

Easy to say! But not always easy to do. In a "Peanuts" comic strip, Lucy gives Linus a lecture on human nature. She draws a heart on a wall with a piece of crayon. Half of the heart she colors red; the other half is left uncolored. "This," she says, "is a picture of the human heart. One side is filled with love, and the other side is filled with hate. These two forces are constantly at war with each other." Linus clutches his chest and says, "I think I know what you mean. I can feel them fighting!"[37]

Who has not had that same conflict between love and hate, compassion and contempt? Yet, Jesus said that we are to love one another (John 13:35), and Peter said that we are to have respect for all men (v. 17).

We will take a giant step in realizing this challenge when we understand that this love for one another is not a feeling but a way of acting. Love is not something you feel. Love is something you do.

Jesus' story of the good Samaritan is an illustration of this kind of love (Luke 10:25-37). Read the story closely and you will discover that Jesus said nothing at all about how the Samaritan felt. Instead, Jesus focused attention on what the man did.

When Jesus commanded us to love our neighbor and when Peter commanded us to honor all men, they did not mean to feel a certain way toward others. Rather, they meant that regardless of how we feel, we are to act toward other people with dignity and respect.

What happens when we honor all men? Men see our good deeds, and they glorify God.

2. *Be a Good Churchman*

To glorify God we must also "love the brotherhood" (v. 17). The present active imperative form is used, meaning "keep on loving the brotherhood." Brotherhood connotes all Christians who are a part of God's family. Love must not only be directed toward our neighbors. We must also love those with whom we share the faith.

Jesus began a forever family in which "There is neither Jew nor Greek, there is neither slave nor free man, there is neither male nor female; for you are all one in Christ Jesus" (Gal. 3:28, NASB). As we love one another in the family of faith, as we exhibit unity in the body of Christ, God will be glorified.

3. *Be a Good Christian*

To glorify God we must "fear God" (v. 17). American historians are familiar with the sermon preached by Jonathan Edwards entitled "Sinners in the Hands of an Angry God." The sermon induced such fear that the congregation shook with emotion. Some trembled. Others fell out in a dead faint. Is that what it means to fear God?

When the Bible says, "The fear of the Lord is the beginning of wisdom" (Ps. 111:10), it does not mean to be paralyzed in terror at the thought of God. Nor does it mean to cower in the presence of God. To fear God means simply to recognize him for who he is and to arrange our lives accordingly. It means to accept God as the Creator, Owner, and Controller of life and to realize that we live all of our lives under his watchful presence. Such fear leads not to anxiety but to action, not to consternation but to consecration.

When Holiday Inns, Inc. decided to build a $55-million casino in Atlantic City, L. M. Clymer, president and chief executive officer of the organization, quit his job in protest. When asked why, he declared, "It is my overriding regard and respect for my Lord Jesus Christ which has led me to this decision."[38] That is a clear picture of the fear of God. Such fear leads to commitment. When others see our commitment, God is glorified.

4. *Be a Good Citizen*

To glorify God, we must also "honor the king" (v. 17). Someone has suggested there are four great lies in American culture today: "Your check is in the mail"; "Of course I will respect you in the morning"; "The delivery is on the truck"; and "I'm from the government, and I'm here to help you." I would add a fifth: "I can be a good Christian without getting involved in government." Separation of church and state does not mean isolation of the Christian from the challenge of citizenship. We can be a good citizen without being a good Christian. It is impossible to be a good Christian without being a good citizen.

The New Testament is permeated with positive pronouncements concerning the responsibilities of the Christian toward the government. All of these pronouncements evolve from the statement of Jesus: "Render to Caesar the things that are Caesar's; and to God the things that are God's" (Matt. 22:21, NASB).

What does being a good citizen have to do with glorifying God? Peter explained in our text: "Submit yourselves for the Lord's sake to every human institution, whether to a king as the one in authority, or to governors as sent by him for the punishment of evildoers and the praise of those who do right. For such is the will of God that by doing right you may silence the ignorance of foolish men. Act as free men, and do not use your freedom as a covering for evil, but use it as bondslaves of God" (vv. 13-16).

In the Sermon on the Mount, Jesus articulated the challenge for every Christian. "Let your light shine before men in such a way that they may see your good works, and glorify your Father who is in heaven" (Matt. 5:16, NASB). Live in such a way that you make God look good! Are you?

2 PETER

61. Holy Mathematics

2 Peter 1:3-8

Jack Gulledge tells of a visit to the home of Mrs. J. O. Williams in Nashville. Her gorgeous garden is decorated with a flower-covered arbor and ornate water fountains. As he strolled through the flower-lined walkways, Gulledge commented, "Mrs. Williams, you must have a green thumb!" "No," she responded, "I have a dirty thumb and a purple knee!"

Growth does not come automatically, in gardens or in Christians. How can Christian growth occur? Peter gave one model for growth in our text. According to Peter, growth comes when we add the proper ingredients to the original factor of faith. Notice how Peter adds things up.

1. *Moral Excellence*

The first factor to add to faith is moral excellence. Both the King James Version and the Revised Standard Version translate the word as *virtue*. In the *New American Standard Bible* the rendering is "moral excellence." After having asked Jesus Christ to come into our life, we are to begin living a life characterized by moral excellence and purity.

This is not a solo proclamation from one book in the New Testament. It is a message that permeates the entire Bible. To Timothy Paul wrote, "Keep yourself pure" (1 Tim. 5:22, RSV). Paul wrote to the Corinthian Christians, "Therefore, having these promises, beloved, let us cleanse ourselves from all defilement of flesh and spirit, perfecting holiness in the fear of God" (2 Cor. 7:1). In his epistle, John wrote, "And everyone who has this hope fixed on Him purifies himself, just as He is pure" (1 John 3:3). Jesus himself said that it is the pure in heart who will see God (Matt. 5:8).

The unanimous testimony of God's Word is that if we really want our life to be used by God, if we really want our life to be productive for him, we have to keep ourselves pure, exemplifying in our life that moral excellence that brings glory to God.

What does this involve?

Moral excellence involves what we do. To attain moral excellence, there are some things we simply must not do. The Bible declares some things wrong for the Christian; they are to be purposely excluded from our life.

Moral excellence also involves what we think. This is why Paul wrote, "Whatever is true, whatever is honorable, whatever is of good repute, if there is any excellence and if anything worthy of praise, let your mind dwell on these things" (Phil. 4:8, NASB).

Moral excellence also involves the things that we expose ourselves to. A group of tourists was going to tour a coal mine one day. When one young lady appeared dressed in a dainty white dress, her friends laughed at her.She turned to the guide and said, "Can't I wear a white dress down into the mine?" The old man returned, "There's nothing to keep you from wearin' a white dress down there, but there'll be considerable to keep you from wearing one back."

The spiritual truth is that when we continually expose ourselves to the filth, and evil, and temptation, and immorality of the world, it will eventually rub off on us. We must be careful about where we go, be careful about whom we associate with, be careful what we read, be careful what we see. What we habitually expose ourselves to will determine the ultimate direction in which our lives go.

2. *Knowledge*

The next factor is knowledge. The Greek word means insight or understanding. Insight and understanding come from study.

One little boy who was promoted from the Preschool department in Sunday School said to his mother, "Mom, I don't see why teacher wasn't promoted, too. She knows 'bout as much as I do." The little boy was closer to the truth than we like to admit. A lot of Christians have limited spiritual knowledge. The reason for limited spiritual knowledge is lack of study.

Can you imagine an effective teacher who never studies in preparing his lesson plan? Can you imagine a good lawyer who does not regularly reexamine his law books? Can you imagine an efficient doctor who does not daily study the newest developments and latest techniques? Of course not. Yet we Christians often think that we can be stars in God's kingdom without disciplining ourselves to study.

The only way we can grow as Christians is to grow in our knowledge of the Lord Jesus Christ. The only way we can grow in knowledge is to study.

3. *Discipline*

The third factor is discipline. The Greek word literally means "holding oneself in." Self-control is the idea connoted by this word.

Many Christians today want growth without growing pains. In our day of soft Christianity and cheap faith we need to hear again the challenge of Jesus in Mark 8:34 where he said, "If anyone wishes to come after Me, let him deny himself, and take up his cross, and follow Me." That's discipline.

What one well-known statistician said about the realm of business, that "the really big men in America have won their spurs by doing what they didn't want to do when they didn't want to do it," is equally true in the spiritual realm. The really big men in the kingdom of God are the ones who have been willing to do what they didn't want to do when they didn't want to do it. If discipline demanded they part company with the crowd, they did it. If discipline demanded forfeiture of some temporary pleasure, they did it. If it meant to pray when they didn't feel like it, they did it. If it meant to love someone who was unlovely, they did it. We cannot do what we want to and grow as a Christian. We must do what God wants us to do. We must add discipline.

4. *Perseverance*

The fourth factor is perseverance. Although the King James Version translates the Greek word *patience*, a more accurate rendering would be perseverance. The word literally means "to remain under." The word speaks of staying power.

Trace the experience of Demas from Philemon 24 to Colossians 4:14 and then to 2 Timothy 4:10, and you will see the pattern of all too many in today's churches: "Demas, Luke, my fellow-workers"; "Demas"; "Demas, having loved this present world, has deserted me."

No matter how talented we are, or how smart we are, or how eager we are at the beginning of our Christian pilgrimage, we will never move toward spiritual maturity unless we are willing to see it through to the end.

5. *Godliness*

The next factor is godliness. Godliness is a quality of oneness with God which comes through prayer. There is no other way to experience godliness than to spend time with God.

E. Stanley Jones has given what could be the testimony of every Christian when he said, "I find myself better or worse as I pray more or less. It works with almost mathematical precision."

There were three experiences in the Scriptures where a person's face glowed with a special divine radiance. In each case the glow came because of time in God's presence. Moses on Sinai (Ex. 34:35), Jesus on the mountain of transfiguration (Matt. 17:2), and Stephen gazing into heaven (Acts 6:15). The glow of God's presence on our face, the quality of godliness in our lives, comes by spending time with God.

6. *Love*

A final, essential factor is love. Peter mentioned two kinds of love—brotherly kindness and that kind of love that became identified with Christians, *agape* love.

How does love affect growth? As we open our lives to others

through genuine love, their experiences are added to our experiences. The result is an expansion of what we are.

When we add all these factors to faith, what is the sum total in our life? Notice the way Peter expressed it: "For if these qualities are yours and are increasing, they render you neither useless nor unfruitful in the true knowledge of our Lord Jesus Christ" (v. 8).

Faith plus moral excellence plus knowledge plus discipline plus perseverance plus godliness plus love equals growth! That is holy mathematics.

1 JOHN

62. Fantastic

1 John 4:9-10

After many years of marriage, when childbearing prospects had been about given up, a couple had a son. The pregnancy was such a huge surprise that the mother cried out, "It's fantastic!" Therefore, the boy was named "Fantastic." In due time, the boy grew up, married, and in later years of his life requested that his wife not put the name *Fantastic* on his tombstone. He explained that he had always disliked the name. When he died, she complied with his request. On the stone she put the dates of his birth and death and this inscription: "In forty years of happy married life he never looked at another woman." And when strangers gazed at his tombstone, they exclaimed, "Fantastic!"

When I read what the Bible says about the love of God, that is the response that erupts from my soul: *Fantastic*. To think that the God of the universe, the God who holds the whole world in his hands loves us is just fantastic.

John focused on this incredible love in the fourth chapter of his first epistle. He said that love comes from God (v. 7). He declared that God is love (v. 8). He stated that God revealed this love (v. 9). And then in verse 10, John described God's love. Two aspects of God's love are made plain in this description.

1. *Seeking Love*

God's love, said John, is a seeking love. God is always the one who takes the initiative. The good news is not that we first loved God, but that God first loved us.

Howard Hendricks wrote of a young man named William who was a fugitive from the police. He had run away with his girl friend because their parents had been trying to break them up. He thought her parents had sent the police after them. What William didn't know was that the ailment he had been seeing the doctor about was diagnosed as cancer shortly after his disappearance. He needed immediate treatment. William was doing his best to allude the police lest he lose his love, while they were doing their best to find him lest he lose his life. He thought they wanted to take his love away from him. On the contrary, they wanted to give back his life to him.[39]

William is representative of every person whose guilt tells him that God is after him to punish him. Man is so desperate to get away from God that he does not understand that God is trying to catch him so that he can save him.

That is why, as beautiful as the story of the prodigal son is, it is not the most descriptive picture of the love of God for sinful man. In the story of the prodigal son (Luke 15), the father is at home, waiting with open arms for his son to return. Although he certainly welcomes his son when he does come, it is more a picture of passive love than active love. The love of God for sinful man, manifested in his activities in history, reflected in the life of Christ, and proclaimed in his Word, is not a passive love but an active love. God's love is more accurately described by the two other parables that Jesus told in Luke 15—of the shepherd who having lost one sheep, immediately went out to look for it and having found it rejoiced, or of the woman who having lost one coin diligently searched for it until she found it.

God's love is a seeking love. It is a love which sought Elijah hiding in a cave, which confronted Moses out in the wilderness, which burst into Isaiah's presence as he worshiped, which found Jonah in the stomach of a great fish, which touched Saul on the way to Damacus.

God's love does not wait until we come to him. He constantly, continuously seeks to come to us. Sometimes when we least expect it, God will tap us on the shoulder, or burst into the darkness of our lives, or knock at our heart's door, or speak to us out of the silent agony of suffering, and he'll say, "I love you, and if you let me I'll change your life." God's love is a seeking love. That's why it is so fantastic.

2. *Saving Love*

God's love is also a saving love. "This is love," John said, "that he sent his son to be the propitiation for our sins." Don't let that word *propitiation* throw you. It means to cover or to take care of. The word comes out of the sacrificial system of John's day. What John is saying is that God's love not only comes to us. It comes to us with the power to change us from what we are into what we should be. It removes the stain of our sin. It lifts the burden of our guilt. It shatters the chains of our bad habits. It sets us free to realize our God-given potential. God's love saves us.

Charles Studd was one of the wealthy aristocrats of England in the last century, an astute and successful businessman. He was, however, totally unconcerned about the things of God. He lost a bet to a man one day and, as a payment for the debt, had to go hear the crude American preacher who was in town. The preacher was Dwight L. Moody. When Studd arrived at the meeting that night, the crowds were so great that he had to sit on the very front row. Studd never took his eyes off of Moody. After the service was over, he said to his friend, "That fellow has just told me everything I have ever done." He went back the next night and the next until finally he decided to turn his life over to Jesus Christ.

Studd lived only two years after that time, but it was said at his funeral that he did more for Christ in two years than most do in twenty. He turned his great mansion into a meeting place for Bible study. He wrote his friends about their spiritual condition and laughed when they replied rudely. He called on his tailor and his shirtmaker and the man from whom he had bought his cigars and spoke of Christ. "All I can say," said the coachman, "is that though there's the same skin, there's a new man on the inside."[40] The truth of John 3:16 reigns in the life of a new man in Christ!

2 JOHN

63. False Spirits

2 John 7

His name was Hawkshaw. He hit our church right out of Nashville and the Grand Old Opry. He had flown in earlier that day on his private jet. He drove eighteen-wheelers in his spare time. He was some kind of guy. Or at least according to him he was. After Hawkshaw had been with us a couple of weeks, one of our men came up to me and asked, "This Hawkshaw. Is he for real?"

There are a lot of folks in the world who are not for real. False "deceivers" is what John called them. John's message is a message for our day: "You can't believe everything you hear." We need to hear that message, because we are usually extremely undiscerning concerning what we believe. Politicians win elections because of that fact. Advertising sells products because of that fact. Charismatic leaders build large followings because of that fact. Newsmen mold public opinion because of that fact. However, the truth touches every area of life: you can't believe everything you hear.

What is true in our day was also true in John's day. He warned in his second epistle that "many deceivers have gone out into the world" (v. 7). Several such false spirits seek to deceive man today.

1. *Self*

First, there is the false spirit of "self." Social critic Tom Wolfe called the 70s the "me decade." Ours is an age when narcissicism, excessive self-love, is common. *Time* magazine declared a few months back: "One difficulty in diagnosing pathological narcissicism is that the whole culture has turned in a narcissistic direction." Self has been placed in the center of our lives. Every decision, every action, every relationship is determined by how it enhances self.

Wayne Dyer has written a national best-seller entitled, *Your Erroneous Zones*. The book begins with this quote from Walt Whitman: "The whole theory of the universe is directed unerringly to one single individual—namely to you." That is one of the spirits of our age. Self-fulfillment is to be our primary goal according to this spirit. But that is a false spirit.

We do, of course, need to recognize our own worth. And we do need to develop a healthy self-image. But the spirit that tells us that self-fulfillment is life's most important goal and that the universe revolves around us is a false spirit.

2. *Sensuality*

There is another false spirit of our day: sensuality. According to this spirit, pleasure is to be our primary goal in life. This is the spirit that urges us to grab for all the gusto we can get. The television is the primary proclaimer of this false message. We in America have accepted it to an alarming degree.

I read an article recently by Dr. John Money, a professor of medical psychology at Johns Hopkins in Baltimore. He said that American society, backed by an outdated moral code, makes teenage sex a mess and therefore messes up our teenagers. The interviewer made the statement, "You still haven't given me the solution to the problem of teenage pregnancy." Dr. Money gave this answer, "The problem is that we make it a problem."[41]

This is a widely accepted view in our day. The problem with modern society is our outdated moral code. The answer is free sex and an unlimited commitment to pleasure. That, too, is a false spirit.

3. *Secularism*

There is a third false spirit in our day: secularism. Secular means having to do with the material world as over against the spiritual world. According to the spirit of secularism, not self nor pleasure but money is to be the primary desire in life.

This spirit has captured our age. Gold has become our god.

The door-to-door salesman who said to the housewife, "Let me show you a little item your neighbors said you couldn't afford," was pandering to this spirit of secularism. Another expression of this spirit is the young lady who said, "I don't want to marry a go-getter but an already-gotter." We have been persuaded to believe that if you have money and the things money can buy, you have everything necessary for a full and meaningful life.

We do, of course, need money to survive in today's world. And it is nice to be able to have the things that money can buy. But the spirit which suggests that material things can satisfy the spiritual longings in man's heart, that temporary possessions can give man an eternal investment is a false spirit.

4. *Summary*

Some in our day say, "Put self in the center and make every decision on that basis." Others say, "Make pleasure your primary aim in life." Others still say, "Make all the money you can, and you'll be happy." All three of those are false spirits. But you ask, "How do we know they are false spirits?" John answered that question in our text. A false spirit is one that contradicts or refuses to acknowledge Jesus Christ. Compare John's statement in 1 John 4:1-3. John concluded that we are to test the spirits by Jesus Christ. He is the revelation of God by which we are to determine the validity of other revelations in our day.

Because of Jesus, we know that the spirit of self is wrong, for he said, "If anyone wishes to come after Me, let him deny himself, and take up his cross, and follow Me. For whoever wishes to save his life shall lose it; but whoever loses his life for My sake and the gospel's shall save it" (Mark 8:34-35, NASB).

Because of Jesus we know that the spirit of sensuality is wrong, for he said, "You have heard that it was said, 'You shall not commit adultery', but I say to you, that everyone who looks on a woman to lust for her has committed adultery with her already in his heart" (Matt. 5:27-28, NASB).

Because of Jesus we know that the spirit of secularism is wrong, for he said, "For what does it profit a man to gain the whole world, and forfeit his soul?" (Mark 8:36, NASB).

Do not believe everything you hear. Test the spirits of this age by the spirit of Jesus.

3 JOHN

64. To Lie or Not to Lie

3 John 3

Picture yourself in a grocery store in the country several decades ago. A woman comes in to buy a chicken for supper. The butcher reaches his hand into the vat of liquid in which he keeps the chickens and pulls one out. When he tells the woman how much it weighs, she says that she needs one a little bigger. This was the last chicken that the butcher had, the only one left in the vat. But the woman doesn't know it. So the butcher drops it into the vat, reaches in like he is fishing around for another one, pulls out the same chicken and tells her that it weighs about six ounces more. The woman pauses. Then she says, "OK, I'll take both of them."

Now that man has a problem. The source of his problem is a common source of our problems today: falsehood. Falsehood and deception have always haunted us. From the time Satan deceived Eve with a lie about the effect of the forbidden fruit (Gen. 3:4-5), man has been tempted to skirt the truth. "To lie or not to lie" is often the question that faces each of us.

1. *The Reason for Falsehood*

Why are we so tempted to lie? Why don't we just tell the truth?

Part of the answer is that we do not like what we are. The basic problem with most of us today is not pride. It is a feeling of inferiority. We do not think we are a somebody. We fear that we are a nobody. In order to build ourselves up before the eyes of others, we often stretch the truth. Read Acts 5:1-10 to see how this was exhibited in the lives of Ananias and Sapphira.

At other times we lie because we do not like what others

are. They are threats to us. In order to bring them down to our level, we spread untruths about them. This was the foundation for the lies of Potiphar's wife about Joseph in Genesis 39:14-18.

Most often lies find their inception in unpleasant situations. It may be fear that arises from a dangerous situation as when Peter lied in Matthew 26:69-75. Or it may be guilt for something we have done. We know that we were wrong, and we are caught. To avoid our responsibility we hide behind a lie. The feeble attempt of Aaron in Exodus 32:1-24 is a good example of this.

Each of these biblical examples has a modern-day counterpart. To enhance our ego we often talk about accomplishments that we never really made. To bring someone else down to our own level, we often spread untruths about that person. To escape guilt or find freedom from unpleasant situations we often fabricate stories. The motives have been the same over the centuries. Only the settings have changed.

2. *The Result of Falsehood*

So what's wrong with a little lie ever now and then? What is a little deception going to hurt?

Consider that question from a biblical point of view. The Bible clearly condemns deception of every kind. The biblical injunctions are both negative and positive at this point.

Negatively, the Bible says that deception and falsehood are wrong. Listen to these random samples. Proverbs 12:22 (KJV) says, "Lying lips are an abomination to the Lord." Exodus 23:1 says, "You shall not utter a false report" (RSV). The practice of using false measures in the marketplace is also strongly condemned (Lev. 19:35-36, Deut. 25:13-15, Prov. 11:1; 16:11, etc.). The New Testament continues this same theme. Christians are exhorted to "let no corrupt communication proceed out of your mouth" (Eph. 4:29, KJV), and to "Lie not one to another" (Col. 3:9, KJV).

The positive support for truth is also evident. We should walk before God in truth (1 Kings 2:4), love truth (Zech.

8:19), rejoice in the truth (1 Cor. 13:6), meditate upon the truth (Phil. 4:8), and speak to one another in truth (Eph. 4:25).

Walking in truth is the theme of John's third epistle. When word came to him that his brethren were walking in truth he rejoiced, for he said, "I have no greater joy than this, to hear of my children walking in the truth" (v. 4, NASB).

Deception is clearly condemned in the Bible and truth is exalted. As a Christian these biblical injunctions must be taken seriously.

A rational approach to the question is also instructive. What would the world be like if everyone lied? Forget for a moment what the Bible says. Think rationally about that possibility. What if everyone lied? What if everyone was deceptive? What kind of world would our world be? Immanuel Kant once said that the basic moral directive in life is to "act in such a way that your conduct can become law universal." Deception is wrong because if it was universally practiced it would throw our world into chaotic confusion.

Consider the question also from a practical point of view. When you lie, does it really do any good? Do you really avoid accepting yourself as you really are, or do you just postpone that acceptance? Do you really bring someone else down to your own level, or do you merely lower yourself even further? Do you really get out of an unpleasant situation by lying, or do you simply multiply the problems? In actual practice, deception causes more problems than it solves.

Jesus had much to say about truth. The climax of Jesus' teaching on truth is found in John 8:32 where he said that the truth will set us free. That is why truth is important. That is why deception is dangerous. Deception binds us in a web of lies. But truth sets us free to be ourselves. It sets us free to let others be themselves. It sets us free to face the situations of life as they really are.

3. *The Remedy for Falsehood*

What is the remedy for falsehood? How can we as Jesus' followers walk in truth?

Recognize deception for what it is, a destructive force in life. Dishonesty does not bring freedom but bondage. It does not enhance life. It inhibits life. Deception is a tool by which the evil one causes confusion in our life and chaos in the world. It is at best a temporary solution. But it is a solution that causes more problems than it solves.

Recognize discipleship for what it is, a commitment to truth in life. Jesus proclaimed that his followers were to live by the truth. This was the upshot of his challenge in Matthew 5:37: "Let what you say be simply 'Yes' or 'No'; anything more than this comes from evil" (RSV). We cannot be followers of the One who is *the truth* and walk in deception. As Jesus came to communicate the truth, so are we to do (John 8:31-32). When you catch yourself in a lie, confess it as a sin before God and claim the forgiveness which he offers (1 John 1:9). Don't let these individual lies develop into the habit of deception.

To lie or not to lie? This question has already been answered for us as Christians. Jesus wants our lives to be characterized by honesty (Matt. 5:37). More than that, he has given to us the Holy Spirit who will help us to know what the truth is (John 16:13). We are, as John expressed it, to walk in truth.

JUDE

65. *Evil Workers Are Coming!*

Jude 17-21

A small, anemic-looking cowboy was hired as a bartender in an old western saloon. The owner of the establishment gave the new bartender only one bit of advice. "If you ever hear that Big John is coming," said the owner, "You'd better drop everything and run for cover." Work proceeded without difficulty for several weeks. Then one day a cowhand rushed in shouting, "Big John is coming! Big John is coming!" The saloon emptied immediately with people going out every door and window. In the rush of the crowd, the bartender was knocked down. By the time he picked himself up, he saw a giant of a man with a black, bushy beard ride up to the saloon on a buffalo using a rattlesnake for a whip. The man tore both doors off the hinges as he came in, flung the snake into the corner of the saloon, and split the bar from one end to the other with a single blow of his massive fist. He picked up the bartender, raised him to within one inch of his face, and demanded, "Give me a drink." Then he threw the bartender down. Nervously, the bartender pushed a bottle to the man. He broke the neck off, downed the contents in one gulp, and smashed the bottle into the mirror. As the gigantic intruder turned to leave, the bartender said meekly, "Do you want another drink?" "Not me," roared the man, "I am getting out of here. Big John's coming!"

We've all been in those situations when we thought Big John was already there, when in reality Big John was still coming. When the going gets tough, what is the Christian to do? Jude suggested four responses to the crucible experiences of life.

1. *Look Back*

Jude encouraged his contemporaries to "remember the words that were spoken beforehand by the apostles of our Lord Jesus Christ" (v. 17, NASB). When the going gets tough in the present, look to the past. Remember what has gone before.

Remember the *warning* that has been given. In Acts 20:29 Paul warned against grievous wolves who would enter the church "not sparing the flock." Paul wrote to young Timothy: "In the latter times some shall depart from the faith, giving heed to seducing spirits, and doctrines of demons" (1 Tim. 4:1, KJV). And again, "In the last days perilous times shall come" (2 Tim. 3:1, KJV). In his epistle, Peter warned, "Beloved, do not be surprised at the fiery ordeal among you, which comes upon you for your testing, as though some strange thing were happening to you; but to the degree that you share the sufferings of Christ, keep on rejoicing; so that also at the revelation of His glory, you may rejoice with exultation" (1 Pet. 4:12-13, NASB). Those who went before us said that there would be days like this. So don't be surprised.

Remember the *word* that has been given. For perilous times, the Bible speaks words of comfort. Jesus promised his disciples (and us), "I will not leave you as orphans" (John 14:18, NASB). Jesus will never leave us without the protection, power, and perspective that a father can give. Jesus will be with us through every experience. Paul built on that promise when he proclaimed to the Philippians: "And my God shall supply all your needs according to His riches in glory in Christ Jesus" (Phil. 4:19, NASB). Paul spoke another word of promise to the Corinthians: "No temptation has overtaken you but such as is common to man; and God is faithful, who will not allow you to be tempted beyond what you are able, but with the temptation will provide the way of escape also, that you may be able to endure it" (1 Cor. 10:13, NASB). When the going gets tough, remember the promises Jesus made. He will be with us. He will supply all our needs. He will provide avenues of escape. Remember these words of promise.

When the going gets tough, look back. Remember the warning of those who preceded us and the word of promise Jesus gave.

2. *Look In*

Then Jude suggested "building yourselves up on your most holy faith; praying in the Holy Spirit" (v. 20). When the going gets tough, look in. Develop a firm foundation of faith on which to stand.

How do we build ourselves up in the faith? The Bible says that we are built up as we desire the Word (1 Pet. 2:2), as we hear the Word (Rom. 10:17), and as we obey the Word (1 John 2:5).

I was interviewing a young seminary graduate for an education position in the church I pastored. He interrupted me to say, "You don't understand, pastor. I don't want to be an education man. I want to be a preacher." I pointed out that his degree was in education instead of theology to which he responded, "I already know all I need to know about the Bible. I got me a degree in education so I'd know how to run a church!"

Many Christians feel they know all they need to know about the Bible. Closer to reality is the statement of the old professor who said, "To study infinity requires eternity." Continuous commitment to the study of God's Word is essential if we are to be built up into the kind of individuals who can keep going when the going gets tough.

3. *Look Up*

Jude gave another suggestion in verse 21. "Keep yourselves in the love of God" (KJV). He did not say to keep loving God. Our love waivers. His focus is upon the love of God which does not waiver. We are to keep ourselves in the sphere of God's love.

A positive example of this principle is Paul's statement to the Philippians. "For to me to live is Christ" Paul said (Phil. 1:21, KJV). What he meant was that his entire life was lived in the realm of God's love as it was revealed in Christ.

A negative example of this principle is Jesus' parable of the prodigal son. The prodigal was still his father's son. He still belonged to him. But he had removed himself from the place where he could enjoy the benefits of his father's love.

How do we keep in the love of God? Jesus answered that question in the intimate communion of his last night with his disciples. "If you keep My commandments," he said, "you will abide in My love" (John 15:10, NASB).

4. *Look Forward*

A fourth suggestion Jude gave is to wait "anxiously for the mercy of our Lord Jesus Christ to eternal life" (v. 21). The Greek word used here is translated in four passages as "waiting anxiously for" and in four passages as "looking for." We are to live in an atmosphere of eager anticipation because we know that when Jesus comes, he will deal with us in mercy, and he will take us to the place he has prepared for us.

Because of some birth defects, the little girl's body was different from those of her friends. The mother protected her as well as she could, but when the girl started to school she was faced by the cruelty that children sometimes express. The girl was in tears when she returned home after the first day. She crawled into her mother's lap and cried, "Mom, why did God make me like this?" The wise mother responded, "Honey, God is not through with you yet."

When the going gets tough, remember that God is not through with you yet. So keep serving the One "who is able to keep you from stumbling, and to make you stand in the presence of His glory blameless with great joy" (v. 24, NASB).

REVELATION

66. The Gifts of Christmas

Revelation 1:5-6

From the beginning, the giving of gifts has been a vital part of the celebration of Christmas. In that first Christmas season, the wise men brought gifts of gold, frankincense, and myrrh to the Christ child. Today, Christmas inevitably focuses our attention on the giving and receiving of gifts. Joy comes when we give the person we love "just what they wanted."

The real gifts of Christmas, however, are not what we give to each other but what Jesus gives to us. Christmas is a celebration of the fact that God gave us something through Jesus Christ.

In the expression of praise in the first chapter of Revelation, this doxology to Christ, John set down in stupendous splendor and sublime simplicity the gifts of Christmas.

1. *Love*

One of the greatest gifts Jesus gives us is the gift of love. But what kind of love is it?

It is an *embracing love.* Notice the order John used in our text. Jesus did not, first of all, liberate us and lift us up to a new life as kings and priests and then decide that he would love us. The love came first. "God commendeth his love toward us, in that, while we were yet sinners, Christ died for us" (Rom. 5:8, KJV). That is the message of Christmas. When we did not deserve it, when we had no right to expect it, when we were yet in our sins, then Jesus loved us and came to us and embraced our lives.

How different from the God-man relationship depicted in other religions. In Islam, the Muslim believer urgently desires to make a pilgrimage to Mecca at least once during his lifetime as part of his search for God. The Buddhist is encouraged to withdraw from humanity and meditate upon his soul until he finds God. The Hindu is challenged to get off the wheel of incarnation through moral living and enter into nirvana, the place of absorption into the divine spirit of the universe.

In every other religion it is man seeking God. In Christianity the message that erupts from that dark Judean night long ago is that God seeks man. His love comes to us where we are. It is an embracing love.

This love is also an *excusing love.* Notice the word that the writer of Revelation used to speak of the love of Christ. It is the word *agape.* There are other Greek words for love, but *agape* love is a special kind of love. *Agape* love is a love that is willing to think the best of us and want the best for us, a love which is willing to wipe out the past and start over with the present. *Agape* love is willing to embrace us today, regardless of what we have done yesterday. It is that kind of love with which Christ loves us.

This love is also an *eternal love.* Notice the tense. The King James Version translates incorrectly, "unto him that loved us." The verb is not in the past tense. It is in the present tense. It should be, "To him who loves us."

Dr. Tregelles, a great Bible scholar who spent his lifetime examining the ancient manuscripts of the Scriptures, established beyond a shadow of doubt that the verb which describes Christ's love for us in this verse is in the present tense. He concluded that this one discovery—that Jesus' love is not in the past tense but in the present tense—was sufficient payment for all of his years of labor.

"To Him who loves us . . . to Him be the glory and the dominion forever and ever."

2. *Liberation*

A second gift of Christmas is liberation. This One who loves us also liberates us from our sins by his blood. The King James Version has "washed us from our sins." This is not what the oldest manuscripts have. The oldest, most reliable manuscripts have the word "loosed" or "liberated" instead of "washed."

This word is used in Matthew 21:2 when Jesus sent his disciples after a donkey in preparation for his triumphant entry into the city of Jerusalem. The Bible says, "They loosed the colt and brought him to Jesus (author's translation)." The same word is used of the woman healed by Jesus in Luke 13:12, (KJV). For eighteen years she had a spirit of infirmity. Consequently, she was in no way able to lift herself up. Jesus said to her, "Woman, you are freed from your sickness," and instantly she was made straight. This same word is used in Acts 2:24 (KJV) to proclaim that Jesus was loosed from the pains of death, and in Acts 22:30 when the Roman officials loosed Paul from the chains in which he had been held captive. Jesus not only loves us. He also liberates us—he sets us loose—from whatever has our life in bondage.

Ironically, in our day when the watchwords are freedom and liberty, man is more in bondage than he has ever been. We were created to expand our consciousness through prayer, to extend our hands in service, to express our thanks with joy, to expend our energies with wisdom, to exemplify our love by deeds. But our prayers have been silenced by our sin, our hands of service bound by our selfishness, our joy eclipsed by our sorrow, our energies stifled by our slothfulness, and our deeds of mercy eliminated by our self-centeredness.

In the Christmas season, we are reminded again of a peace we do not experience and a joy we do not feel and a brotherhood that we do not have. More so than at any other time of the year, Christmas confronts us with the reality of our bondage. Above the muffled carols and the mock hilarity of the season, there sounds the agonizing cry of the multitudes in their sin: "Wretched man that I am! Who will set me free from the body of this death" (Rom. 7:24, NASB)? Who will liberate us from our bondage? He will do it, says the writer of Revelation. This one who is the faithful witness, the firstborn from among the dead, the ruler of the kings of this earth—this one named Jesus who loves us with a love that is eternal, he will loose us from our sins by his blood.

3. *Lift*

There is yet a third gift that Jesus gives us. He loves us. He liberates us. And then, he lifts us up. Listen to the way the writer of Revelation puts it, "To Him who loves us, and released us from our sins by His blood, and He has made us to be a kingdom, priests to His God and Father." What he is saying is that Jesus not only saves us from something. He also saves us to something. He liberates us so that we might live as kings and priests.

In a message J. Sidlow Baxter preached, this idea was beautifully expressed. Baxter said that when God delivered Israel from bondage there were two movements, the movement out of Egypt, and the movement into Canaan. All of the children of Israel moved out of Egypt. But not all of them moved into the Promised Land. Some died in the wilderness. The same thing can be said of Christianity. In the liberation that Jesus effects there are two movements, the movement out of the Egypt of our sin and the movement into the Canaan of abundant living. Every Christian has moved out of the Egypt of sin. But not every Christian has moved into the Canaan of abundant living. All do not know the glory of royal existence. All do not know the joy of sweet fellowship. All do not know the thrill of victory. All have not yet entered into the Promised Land. But that is what Jesus wants for us. He wants to lift us up to a new level of existence where ecstatic joy, enduring peace, enervating power, and exhilarating victory become the everyday experiences of our lives.

The glorious message of Christmas, the pulsating promise of our text, is that there is much more in life than we have experienced. Jesus doesn't want us to just exist. He wants us to live as kings and priests, reigning with him and enjoying his presence. He wants to lift us up to a new level of living.

NOTES

New Testament

1. Quoted by Robert Raines, "A Revolution of Understanding" in *What's a Nice Church Like You Doing in a Place Like This?* (Waco, Texas: Word Books, 1972), p. 116.

2. John A. MacArthur, Jr., *The Church - the Body of Christ* (Grand Rapids, Mich.: Zondervan Publishing House, 1973), p. 22.

3. Quoted in Luther Joe Thompson, *Through Discipline to Joy* (Nashville, Tenn.: Broadman Press, 1966), p. 118.

4. Nels Ferré, *Strengthening the Spiritual Life* (New York: Harper & Row, 1951), p. 181.

5. Ibid; p. 195.

6. R. Earl Allen, *Jesus Loves Me* (Nashville, Tenn.: Broadman Press, 1979), pp. 60-61.

7. J. C. Pollock, *Hudson Taylor & Maria* (McGraw-Hill Book Company, Inc., 1962), p. 169.

8. William Barclay, *The Gospel of John*, Vol. 2, Revised Edition (Philadelphia: The Westminster Press, 1975), p. 168.

9. William Barclay, *The Promise of the Spirit* (Philadelphia: The Westminster Press, 1960), p. 35.

10. James P. Wesberry, *Evangelistic Sermons* (Nashville, Tenn.: Broadman Press, 1973), p. 67.

11. Eugenia Price, *What Is God Like?* (Grand Rapids, Mich.: Zondervan Publishing House, 1973), p. 3.

12. W. Herschel Ford, *Simple Sermons on the Great Christian Doctrines* (Nashville, Tenn.: Broadman Press, 1951), p. 12.

13. *The Dallas Morning News*, April 6, 1975.

14. David Haney, *The Idea of the Laity* (Grand Rapids, Mich.: Zondervan Publishing House, 1973), pp. 46-47.

15. John C. Pollock, *Foreign Devil in China* (Grand Rapids, Mich.: Zondervan Publishing House, 1971), p. 54.

16. John Claypool, Sermon preached at Crescent Hill Baptist Church, Louisville, Kentucky.

17. Frank E. Gaebelein, ed. *The Expositors Bible Commentary*, Vol. 10 (Grand Rapids, Mich.: Zondervan Publishing House, 1978), p. 409.

18. Landrum P. Leavell, *Sermons for Celebrating* (Nashville, Tenn.: Broadman Press, 1978), p. 93.

19. C. Welton Gaddy, *Profile of a Christian Citizen* (Nashville, Tenn.: Broadman Press, 1974), p. 17.

20. Arthur Porritt, *John Henry Jowett* (George H. Doran Co., 1924), p. 238.

21. Leslie B. Flynn, *How to Save Time in the Ministry* (Nashville, Tenn.: Broadman Press, 1966), p. 43.

22. *Quote*, Vol. 80, p. 306.

23. John S. Bonnell, *The Practice and Power of Prayer* (Philadelphia: Westminster Press, 1954), p. 57.

24. *Pulpit Digest*, March-April, 1980, p. 38.

25. Luther Joe Thompson, *Through Discipleship to Joy* (Nashville, Tenn.: Braodman Press, 1966), p. 44.

26. James E. McReynolds, *America's No. 1 Drug Problem*(Nashville, Tenn.: Broadman Press, 1977) p. 112.

27. Walter B. Knight, *Knight's Treasury of Illustrations* (Grand Rapids, Mich.: Wm. B. Eerdmans Publishing Co., 1963), p. 443.

28. D. T. Niles, "What Is the Church For?" in *20 Centuries of Great Preaching*, Vol. XII, Clyde E. Fant, Jr. and William M. Pinson, Jr. (Waco, Texas: Word Books, 1971), p. 209.

29. James E. Carter, "When an Ordinary Person Does Extraordinary Things" in *Award Winning Sermons*, Vol. 1 (Nashville, Tenn.: Broadman, 1977), p. 69.

30. A. D. R. Polman, *The Word of God According to St. Augustine* (Grand Rapids, Mich.: Wm. B. Eerdman's Publishing Co., 1961), p. 67.

31. Harry Emerson Fosdick, *The Hope of the World* (New York: Harper & Brothers, 1933), p. 157.

32. Helen Smith Shoemaker, *I Stand by the Door* (NY: Harper & Row, 1967), p. 77.

33. Cecil G. Osborne, *The Art of Becoming a Whole Person* (Waco, Tex.: Word Books, 1978), p. 55.

34. William Barclay, *A Spiritual Autobiography* (Grand Rapids, Mich.: Wm. B. Eerdmans Publishing Co., 1975), p. 36.

35. Kenneth S. Wuest, *Wuest's Word Studies*, Vol. 2 (Grand Rapids, Mich.: Wm. B. Eerdmans Publishing Co., 1974), p. 212.

36. Webster's *New World Dictionary*, 1972 Edition (Nashville, Tenn.: The Southwestern Company, 1969), p. 319.

37. Robert L. Short, *The Gospel According to Peanuts* (Richmond, Va.: John Knox Press, 1965), pp. 39-40.

38. *Quote*, Vol. 77, p. 495.

39. Howard Hendricks, *Say It with Love* (Wheaton, Ill.: Victor Books, 1972), p. 14.

40. John C. Pollock, *Moody* (New York: MacMillan Co., 1963), p. 162.

41. *The Pensacola News-Journal*, August 31, 1980, p. 6*c*.

EPILOGUE

From Cover to Cover
  The deed has been done,
A sermon for each book,
  Now you have at least one.

The outlines are clear,
  The illustrations are light;
May you find them helpful
  On some Saturday night.

The sermons are given
  For preachers to use,
But the message is also
  For those in the pews.

The Bible does speak
  To man's every need;
His words will bring life
  If his challenges we heed.

From Cover to Cover
  This is God's Word;
May the Lord bless these sermons
  Wherever they're heard.